Praise from the Cave

CaveTime has brought me peace and structure. Before CaveTime I only *showed up* when I needed something. Definitely a one-way street. But since starting CaveTime, I am having a closer walk with God, and He has blessed that by meeting my needs, often before I even ask them!

—Jim

Every morning my son (10) gets up at 6 a.m., even on the weekends, just to spend time with me before everyone else. A while back my wife challenged me to use this time well, so this month we used *The Sling* as the first part of our morning. There were many moments for great discussions on how the stones (Worship, Prayer, Word, etc.) can be used in our lives. It brought the Word to life for him. While we studied the stone of Worship, it clicked with him that every action in our life can be worship to God, whether work, fun, or interaction with others, bringing Colossians 3:23–24 to life.

I found myself challenged and reread a number of caves on my own because it hit areas that I need to grow in. We all need to learn to use these stones to slay our giants.

—Kyle

I feel that I can safely say that I am speaking on behalf of all men who attended our retreat this year in saying thanks for leading us and making this a very remarkable life-changing event. I've been to many men's events where the guys just clam up, but something about turning the lights down and being led into that Cave prayer opened up the guys' hearts and spirits very quickly. And genuinely.

Amazing, really.

—Brad, Men's Minister

Jeff says, "If you have the X and Y chromosomes, you are a man." It is amazing how I thought I had to achieve something first.

—Tom

THE SLING

ESSENTIAL TRAINING FOR MEN OF GOD

THE SLING

5 STONES TO MAKE EVERY MAN A GIANT SLAYER

BY JEFF VOTH

HONOR NET
PUBLISHERS
Sapulpa, OK

Published by HonorNet Publishers

HONOR✚NET
P U B L I S H E R S

P.O. Box 910
Sapulpa, OK 74067
Website: honornet.net

Illustrations by designsbyleander@yahoo.com

WANTED

GIANT SLAYERS.
NO EXPERTISE REQUIRED.
STONES PROVIDED. INQUIRE WITHIN.

ACKNOWLEDGMENT

The process that created *The Sling* has been a new one for me. While the other books I have written were done the old-school way (I hammered out a manuscript, submitted it to an editor, rewrote, refined, and then rewrote again), this book has been the result of a collaborative effort between myself and my friend, editor, author, and publisher, Jake Jones. Jake and I have known each other for over thirty years. We've laughed together, gone on missions trips together, argued with each other, and have continued showing up to live out the concepts about which this book speaks. In my opinion this qualifies him to do the amazing and powerful job that he did on *The Sling*. He got into my head, assimilated, created, synthesized, and honed out this powerful tool that is based upon my book *CaveTime*. In *The Sling*, Jake takes the concepts presented in *CaveTime* and breaks them into smaller, palatable chunks. He makes them doable for any and every guy. This is exactly what I told him I wanted to do . . . and he did it . . . we did it. And I am grateful. Thank you, Jake.

So engage with this thing. It was written for you. It was written to help you show up, show up, and show up again, despite getting shot at by the hordes of enemies that your culture will launch at you. Some will feel like intimidating giants sent to shame you, bring fear to you, and kill you. But you, possessor of the X and Y chromosomes, are a man. In fact you're *the* man, and all you need is a weapon…all you need is a sling. Will you pick up this one?

CONTENTS

Intimidating Giants

by Jeff Voth

*Intimidating giants, you will see
how bigger targets they can be.
Stupid, dumb, clumsy, mean.
Perfect prey for my sling.
Porn, shame, lust, pride.
Stumbling idiots, too big to hide.
Worship, prayer, word, and brothers.
Send them running to their mothers.*

PREFACE

I start my book *CaveTime* with the words *Man is under assault.* That is it in a nutshell. Take out the man, and so much of society crumbles. The first act of Satan in the Garden of Eden was to assault the man. His strategy has not changed. The back cover of the *CaveTime* book reads:

> When David was under assault and mere steps ahead of death, he escaped to a place that was familiar to him—the cave, a place of refuge. As a shepherd boy, the cave was where he heard the voice of the Lord, wrote songs and poems, and received his courage, strength, and boldness to kill the lion, the bear, and Goliath. Overcome by the assaults of debt, distress, and discontentment, the greatest warriors of the day were also searching for a refuge—a place where they could find their strength, honor, and bare their souls without judgment. They found refuge and safety in the cave. Something happened in the cave, because later they were referred to as Mighty Men.
>
> Today men are under assault. Blitzed by cultural and spiritual expectations to succeed, most men feel they must present themselves as the perfect man with everything under control. They are defined by jobs, titles, bank accounts, houses, and cars. As husbands, fathers, and spiritual leaders, men are expected to instantly have all the answers. Believing the lie of the enemy of their soul, they become isolated, fearing they won't measure up. Men

need a refuge, a place of safety, a place of escape. Come to the
cave...God is waiting for you there.

Like David, I was driven to the cave by the cares of life. And there it
happened. The Lord revealed to me a key aspect of David. David, when faced
with the giants of his life (I say giants because it is common belief that Goliath
had four giant brothers), picked up five smooth stones from the brook on his
way to meet those giants. Undoubtedly it was something he had done thousands of time before. As a shepherd, his main tools of defense in protecting
the sheep were the stones he would carefully select and his sling. He was a
master slinger. He had honed his skill with the sling to such an extent that a
common stone from a stream became a deadly tool to vanquish the giants that
threatened his life, family, and existence. He had practiced his entire young
lifetime for this moment.

As we read in Samuel 17, he and he alone would stand against all the
accusations, taunting, and vulgar threats from the giant that cursed everything he stood for. I don't think the stones he picked up that day in the valley
of Elah were just any stones. I think David knew what shape, size, and weight
the stones needed to be to be most effective as deadly missiles in his sling of
hemp. The stones had been lying at the bottom of the brook perhaps for 100
years, being shaped and smoothed by the water for just this moment. They
were still just stones...until David carefully selected them based on their merit
and placed them into his pouch.

I can see David not walking but running towards Goliath. As his pace quick-
ened, he could hear the taunting getting louder and louder. 1 Samuel 17:40–51
records the events.

*40 Then he took his staff in his hand, chose five smooth stones from
the stream, put them in the pouch of his shepherd's bag and, with his
sling in his hand, approached the Philistine.*

⁴¹*Meanwhile, the Philistine, with his shield bearer in front of him, kept coming closer to David.* ⁴²*He looked David over and saw that he was little more than a boy, glowing with health and handsome, and he despised him.* ⁴³*He said to David, "Am I a dog, that you come at me with sticks?" And the Philistine cursed David by his gods.* ⁴⁴*"Come here," he said, "and I'll give your flesh to the birds and the wild animals!"*

⁴⁵*David said to the Philistine, "You come against me with sword and spear and javelin, but I come against you in the name of the LORD Almighty, the God of the armies of Israel, whom you have defied.* ⁴⁶*This day the LORD will deliver you into my hands, and I'll strike you down and cut off your head. This very day I will give the carcasses of the Philistine army to the birds and the wild animals, and the whole world will know that there is a God in Israel.* ⁴⁷*All those gathered here will know that it is not by sword or spear that the LORD saves; for the battle is the LORD's, and he will give all of you into our hands."*

⁴⁸*As the Philistine moved closer to attack him, David ran quickly toward the battle line to meet him.* ⁴⁹*Reaching into his bag and taking out a stone, he slung it and struck the Philistine on the forehead. The stone sank into his forehead, and he fell facedown on the ground.*

⁵⁰*So David triumphed over the Philistine with a sling and a stone; without a sword in his hand he struck down the Philistine and killed him.*

⁵¹*David ran and stood over him. He took hold of the Philistine's sword and drew it from the sheath. After he killed him, he cut off his head with the sword.*

This has always been one of my favorite scriptures. Even more so since I was driven to the cave by the cares of life. I love in verses 48 and 49 how David reaches into his pouch as he runs and takes out a stone (carefully selected, I might add), places it into his trusty sling, and—honed through years and thousands of practice slings—sends it towards the head of the giant. It sank into his forehead. Yeah it did. A common stone, chosen from a brook, turned into a weapon and killed a giant. Now that's what I'm talkin' about!

As I had my first CaveTime experience, the Lord began to show me that He had created very specific stones that I could use in my sling in order to slay the giants that assaulted me in my life. Over the years of practicing CaveTime, I have carefully selected—like David—five stones that every man should not only have in his pouch, but be very skilled in using in his sling to kill the giants of his life. They are:

Stone One: Show Up
Stone Two: Worship
Stone Three: Prayer
Stone Four: Word
Stone Five: Community

I originally wrote this as just a manual to go along with my book *CaveTime.* It quickly became a book that could stand alone. *The Sling* is still a great companion and manual to *CaveTime,* but unlike a regular manual, it can stand alone. I realized that the five stones were stones that every man should have in order to battle the giants of his life. I wanted any man to be able to come to a cave of his brother or pick up this book and get the five stones he needed to slay the giants he is facing.

As you get into the book, you will quickly realize that this is not the typical manual or Bible study. I don't do well with studies that rely on memorization and reading. You start with good intentions, get into the third or fourth week, and then cram the night before you meet with the boys so you feel like you are participating. Then before you get to the middle of it, you drop out, adding another layer of shame to your mask.

Like most men, I want to be where the action is. If *The Sling* is an action movie, you are the lead character and hero. This manual is about you *doing.*

I give you the ammo, you shoot the bad guys. You're Rooster Cogburn in *True Grit* with the reins in your teeth, a six-shooter in one hand, and a Winchester in the other.

> [*Rooster confronts the four outlaws across the field*]
>
> **Ned Pepper:** What's your intention? Do you think one on four is a dogfall?
>
> **Rooster Cogburn:** I mean to kill you in one minute, Ned. Or see you hanged in Fort Smith at Judge Parker's convenience. Which'll it be?
>
> **Ned Pepper:** I call that bold talk for a one-eyed fat man.
>
> **Rooster Cogburn:** Fill your hands, you son of a b . . . ![1]

It's all about you practicing until it is yours. I give you the stones, show you how to sling them, then the rest is up to you. You practice, hone your skills, and go kill your giants. Stand between life and death for your family, brothers, and all those you love. I don't want *The Sling* to be a manual or book you read or a Bible Study you participated in. I want it to be a life you live. Not just today, but every day for the rest of your life. You have heard that if you give a man a fish, he eats for a day. If you teach him *how* to fish, he will eat for a lifetime. I want you to be a giant killer. Not for a day, but for a lifetime. Spend the next twelve caves with me, and at the end you will be a giant killer!

Slingers, are you ready? Let's get some stones and kick some giant devil booty. (Yeah, I said it.) Are you with me?

Caveman, Slayer of Giants, and Slinger,

INTRODUCTION
THE LAYOUT

I want to explain how the caves are laid out to give you a better understanding of what to expect and what is expected of you. I have tried to keep it really simple, and I have created a format that you will follow for twelve weeks or twelve months. Some might like to light it up and do a cave each week and burn right through it, no problem. Others might want to take a month to go through a cave or do two caves in a month. That works also. Remember, the main point is to make it a lifestyle. Why go through a study if it doesn't take root in your life? I personally think doing it in six months or a year is a great way to make sure you are practicing what you preach.

Caves

I have broken each section into what I call a cave. There are twelve caves no matter the time frame in which you choose to do them. I ask you to come to the twelve caves with me and emerge a mighty man...a giant slayer.

Cave One

Cave One is not like the other caves which cover the stones. It is just an introduction to what to do with your CaveTime. It's full of good information to get your head in the game. I speak throughout the whole book as if we were sitting by a fire, talking as brothers. It is what I envision David and the mighty men doing. Something happened in the cave, for they emerged as mighty men. That is the goal...emerging as mighty men to slay the giants in our lives. To cover, restore, and take back that which threatens our lives, our families, and all that we hold dear. We are Slingers.

Caves Two–Eleven

The next ten caves are divided up into two caves per stone. As an example, caves two and three cover the stone of Show Up and so on. The first cave of each stone is called Stone Time, and the second cave is called Sling Time. Since there are five stones, you will have two caves per stone which gives you the next ten caves. Following is how each cave is laid out.

Stone Time

In each Stone Time, I give you the attributes of the stone, including scripture, and ways to make it a part of your giant-killing arsenal. It is a time of study and learning.

Dressed to Kill—War Zone

Make no mistake about it. Life is war. This section helps you prepare for the battle the enemy is waging against your soul. The stone is a weapon used to vanquish the enemy. The Dressed to Kill section helps with the strategy you need to defeat your foe. We are not skipping rocks across the pond. We are turning stones into deadly projectiles by placing them into our slings. With these stones we are prepared for war.

Stone

This is where we discuss the stone, its attributes, and the value of having it in our pouch. I give you one or two key Study Scriptures and discuss why this stone is important. Each Stone Time might look a little different depending on the stone.

Stone in Fright

In this section, I give you an example of a situation that is missing the stone. It might be a personal, historical, or biblical situation that shows how the stone was not used. Sometimes I was too afraid to stand up and use the stone, thus the word Fright. Failure is as much a part of learning as success. We learn from both, so I thought it vitally important to include this.

Stone in Flight

In this section, we give you an example of what it looks like when the stone is used correctly. It might be a personal, historical, or biblical story that shows how the stone was used when it was put in the sling and let fly. Thus the word Flight. This shows you what happens when the stone is used in a sling, flying toward its mark.

Sling Time

Following each Stone Time is Sling Time. When a stone is merged with the sling, it becomes a deadly weapon. Sling Time is the second study of each stone and is about you putting into practice what you have learned. Why learn something if you never use it? The goal is not to be perfect or hit all of your targets. The goal is to start slinging. What you practice you become. If you can start slinging, you will continue to sling. This cave starts with several questions and thoughts, and the rest is up to you. You have space to write the successes and failures of your cave. This is where taking a little more time to go through the manual makes sense. Instead of having just a week to start practicing slinging the stone, you have two weeks or a month. The more you sling, the more it becomes a part of who you are.

Stone Time is on me to train and equip you with the tools you need. Sling Time of each stone is on you. It is when you write the story on the walls of your cave. I like to call it hieroglyphics. The goal is not to be perfect, just be in the game. Start making the stones a part of your life.

Cave Twelve

The last cave can take one week or one month. I don't care. It is a time to go back over all of your stones and reflect on how you can make them a part of your life each and every day. Some guys like to go back over what they have written, others want to focus on where they need to improve. Just as CaveTime needs to be a vital part of your life, the stones need to be put into practice in order for them to be a natural part of your life. I feel that I could go through this study every year and see growth in how I use the stones.

WELCOME TO THE CAVE

In this cave I want you to go over some preliminary material to prepare for your Stone and Sling Times. Read over the following material and think and pray about the next twelve caves and what you desire to receive and accomplish once you emerge from the cave. If you are doing it in a group setting, discuss ways to keep each other accountable as well as provide support throughout the study.

I Don't Like Manuals

Many men (okay most) don't really like working through a workbook or study manual. It typically means you fill in the blanks in response to questions that you are supposed to remember from the book that you read or are going through. I have never finished one of these studies. I always end up feeling like I'm back in school filling out a worksheet. I am sure they have their purpose, but I want this to be different, so it will look different. These are twelve studies that relate to the five stones we go over in *CaveTime*, the book.

The goal is singular and simple. You are not doing this manual study to get good credits from your wife or buddies. This is not about something you do, it is about who you are. They say that if you do something for seven to eight weeks, it becomes a habit. I want these stones to become as much a part of your life as going to work, eating, or sleeping. Once they become ingrained into your lifestyle, they will become pillars of your masculinity. The foundation is important, and these are meant to be foundational in your CaveTime, personal walk with God, and other masculine relationships. As a result, they will spill over into your relationships with your spouse and family.

We want these to be principles that you live by. It can and will look different for each man in the cave. I have provided some guidelines, but I encourage you to make it your own. Bottom line is when you finish this study—and the first goal is to make sure you do—it becomes a part of who you are . . . automatically. In order for that to happen, much of what you are going to go over is not just reading in the book. I am going to challenge you to actually DO something. Actually most of this should be about DOING and not sitting on the sidelines. That is the whole purpose of Sling Time. It is how you kill giants. More will happen when you get in the arena than just sitting in the stands. For me I think that summarizes what most studies have been for me. Sitting in the stands watching. I know that the best way for you to learn the stone of Show Up is, well, for you to actually do it. You can read, which is cool, but to go out and Show Up for your wife, kid, or brother will do more for you than anything. Practice what you preach, my dad always said.

I would much rather go fishing than read about it. Reading is fine for when you actually can't get out on the water. But nothing beats standing on the shore of a small mountain stream or glacier lake and getting the line wet. Now that is showing up, my friend! Once you experience that, nothing will satisfy but the real thing. And so it shall be with this manual. I want you to do what we are talking about, and when we are done, you won't have to memorize what you went over like a test in humanities. You will have put into practice the principle and it will be a part of who you are. You won't have to try to implement the stones—they will be ingrained into your DNA.

May heaven resound with the feats that are accomplished by men (us) who dare to show up, worship up, pray up, word up, and band up with a group of brothers by our side.

Rules of the Cave

Hopefully you will find yourself in a cave with other men. Whether you are doing this study with others, by yourself, or a combination of both (which is what I recommend), there are three rules that I would suggest you live by. They are simple but extremely important.

1. What happens in the cave stays in the cave.

I know of no other thing that can kill what God wants to do in a cave or in a group of men quicker and easier than loose lips. Honesty is a by-product of trust. In order for me to feel free to be vulnerable, I have to trust those with whom I am confiding. This takes time to develop. This is the one time it is okay NOT to tell your wife something. If new guys are constantly coming in and out of a cave or men's group, men will not open up. What happens in the cave stays in the cave. Honesty, forthrightness, and true companionship will develop as trust grows. There is this underlying thought that we are only talking about the act of confessing our biggest sins when we talk masculine accountability. I am not. It includes this, of course, but I am talking more about sharing our dreams, fears, troubles, struggles, anxieties, and prayer needs. I am talking about the lost art of masculine friendship.

2. Be truthful.

If all the answers to the questions are what I call "textbook," then someone is not being truthful. In a group setting, if everyone has had a great week, then let me say that it will have been the first time. It is okay and truthful to say, "I didn't have my CaveTime this week," or "my wife made me so mad yesterday." Or . . . well, you get the idea. Truthfulness is being real. Everything in our culture demands that we present well. It is a major part of our assault. We are blitzed by cultural and spiritual expectations to succeed. We carry the lie that if anyone knew how we really felt, or who we really are, they would not accept or like us. So we continue to wear our masks day in and day out until we don't even know ourselves. Most men not only struggle with being truthful with others, but most of all to themselves. You must be able to be honest and truthful with yourself about yourself. This is one of the greatest assets of being in the cave with men who love you enough to be honest. When the enemy of your soul speaks lies, they speak truth. When you don't see those things in your character that hinder you, they will be honest in love. Truthfulness is a *must* in the cave.

3. The cave is a circle.

In the cave there needs to be some leadership, but not like the typical class-room setting. The cave does not work well when there is one guy acting as the teacher and the rest are pupils. So much in our lives is structured like that. In the Native American culture, there were elders, but they always met in a circle. In a circle there is no head and no tail. Everyone faces each other and has equal footing to speak. You don't have to meet in a circle, of course, but I am saying that every voice needs to be heard. The pastor needs to be in a cave but not acting as the pastor of the cave. He needs the companionship just like all the other men. Strong, honest, truthful men respect this. I know there needs to be coordination for the meeting time of the cave, the flow of ministry etc., but I consider that coordination. What I am trying to convey is that every caveman needs to feel a part. No one person should always dominate the time with their voice, opinions, or needs. Bring what you have and take what you need.

A Stone is Just a Stone

I think it was really cool how David chose the five stones out of a creek bed. He was on his way to meet Goliath. Notice he was on his way to Show Up, and along the way he picked up five stones. What made the stones special?

Nothing. I am sure out of the thousands of times he had used his sling, he had criteria for the type of stones that would work best as projectiles in his homemade sling. My point is they were just stones until he picked them up. They had been lying there in the creek bed for countless years getting smooth by the rushing water over them. Their value or use became evident only when David chose them, put them in his pouch, and headed towards his destiny. Without the sling they were just stones.

There is a point here. The five stones that we are going to cover in this manual will not have any value until you actually use them. You have to put them in the sling and let them fly. I am sure that when David first picked up his sling as a toddler, the stones he let fly were not all that accurate. He started out missing the target more than hitting it. Gradually, with practice, he got closer and closer to his target. By the time he was totally responsible for being the shepherd of the herds, he expected to hit his target—every time. So shall it be with your use of the stones. There is no way of just skipping from beginner to expert in anything. Practice makes perfect. They will only be stones, even in your pouch, until you choose to step out and use them.

I imagine David started out hitting trees and boulders with his slingshot as a young boy. Maybe he tried to knock a small rock off another boulder. He then probably graduated to small game such as hares or birds. When it came time to really protect, he had no problem trusting his aim on the lion and bear. There is no way he could have started on the lion and bear. I am sure it would have been tragic. With confidence and practice, he honed his skill to move from a beginner to an expert. You get the point here, don't you? The stones never changed! They were the same. Probably the same kind of sling, too. The only thing that changed was the continual practice of choosing stones, choosing to put them in the sling, and choosing to let them fly with purpose. A stone is just a stone until you place it into a sling and level it towards its mark. As you begin to show up, begin to worship, begin to pray, begin to devour

God's Word, and as you learn to be in community with other brothers, you will go from a beginner to an experienced warrior that God can use.

Accuracy Beats Strength

Another aspect that I want to share with you is the principle of common. I don't know why, but we men want to swing for the fence every time we get up to bat. There is that testosterone thing within us that when we stand over that little white ball, we want to pulverize it. We feel more stoked from hitting a 300-yard drive than we do sinking a three-foot putt. They both count the same. We want to hit home runs and 300-yard drives more than we want to be accurate.

I have a friend who once shared with me a lesson he learned from his grandfather. His grandfather loved to play golf. He got on the course every chance he could. As my friend grew, he was able to hit the ball further and further. At the same time, his grandfather was losing strength due to age. He expected to be able to beat his grandfather since he was able to it the ball longer and harder than he ever had before. One day his grandfather showed up with only a putter, wedge, and 7 iron. He had several balls in his pocket and no golf bag. He said, "Gramps, where are your clubs?" His grandfather replied that he had all the clubs he needed and wagered lunch on it. His grandfather played eighteen holes using only three clubs and beat his grandson. My friend learned a valuable lesson that day. Strength and muscle don't score without accuracy. Gramps did not hit the ball very far off the tee, but the years of honing his skill made him accurate. One hundred fifty yards down the middle of the fairway beats 300 yards in the woods every day.

As we learn to put our stones into play, don't look for the home run or 300-yard drive. Look for the base hits and three-foot putts. Zechariah 4:10 tells us not to equate small with bad.

¹⁰Do not despise these small beginnings, for the Lord rejoices to see the work begin, to see the plumb line in Zerubbabel's hand." (NLT)

The Lord will rejoice when you start to put slinging the stones into practice. He knows that once you being something, once you Show Up, things will begin to happen. Your accuracy will improve, you will hit your target, and you will learn to trust God and His working through you to bring hope, victory, and peace to those you come in contact with.

Throughout the rest of Cave One, go over the precepts you have just read to make sure they are in your spirit as you get ready to launch into the next ten caves. The following pages are for you to express in writing what you expect from your CaveTime experience.

1. What additional precepts do you want to add?

_____

_____

_____

_____

_____

_____

_____

_____

_____

_____

_____

_____

_____

_____

_____

2. What are some areas of your life that you want to see God do a miracle?

_____

_____

_____

_____

_____

_____

_____

_____

_____

_____

_____

_____

_____

_____

3. Are there any things that you want to add or subtract from
   your life during these next twelve caves (i.e. no TV, weight
   loss, getting into shape, reading a book, writing in a journal)?

_____

_____

_____

_____

_____

_____

_____

_____

_____

_____

_____

_____

_____

4. Ask God to give you a Word for this time. What word (or phrase) do you want to be written on the cave from this time?

_____

_____

_____

_____

_____

_____

_____

_____

_____

_____

_____

_____

_____

SHOW UP

"Men of God.

We are to be men of God. When under attack and when at peace. Make no mistake. As sure as you hear my voice, you will be attacked. War will find you.

Life itself is infested with these battles—big and small, internal and external. King David was under assault on just about every level. His job, his family, his friends, his very life…all were under threat.

If you're a man, at some point you will experience the assault. It can hit on many levels: spiritually, emotionally, and physically. Then what are we to do to escape? I don't have to tell you that it's not in the strength of your arm or the power of your fist that this war is won. We can act stronger than we are, we can claim nothing can defeat us; but when the sun goes down and the crowds have left, we know that without our God we're just a man.

At these times of assault, we're called to **escape**. Or should I say… Show Up. We seek our Maker, and we find Him in solitude. Real solitude. We must choose to do this on a personal level. We choose to take control. How long will we go on saying we tried?

The time is now. The first step is to simply SHOW UP."

CAVE TWO

STONE TIME: SHOW UP

Group Note

Show the video clip of the Show Up stone. Have everyone read the following principles and discuss their thoughts and challenges. Discuss which areas you need to focus on for the stone.

Stone One, as you know by now, is Show Up. At this point I assume you get it. Otherwise you would not be sitting here reading this manual. You are showing up. You are committed. You are resolute in the improvement of your spiritual walk, and you want things with God to be different enough that they spill over into your relationships with your spouse, children, other family members, and those you do life with.

Dressed to Kill—War Zone

Know this. Since you have decided to make your move, the enemy of your soul will make his. Since you have drawn a line in the sand and stepped up to it toe-to-toe, it is quite possible that all hell will break loose to keep you from showing up. The enemy knows that nothing good can happen if you are not in the game. If he can keep you in the stands, you're off the field. Football 101. The opposing offense cannot score points if they are not on the field. Your offense is your best defense. Extra hours at work, busted pipes, car problems, child behavioral issues…all will come up out of nowhere with one purpose. To keep you from showing up for CaveTime and making these stones a part of your foundation.

That is why showing up is so important. No matter what, you have to show up. Even if you don't feel like it, even if you have no spiritual thoughts, prayers, or positive energy…still show up. I have had guys going through divorce who did nothing but come to my cave and lay on the floor for months. No input or participation, but I made sure they showed up. God honors that. He always does. For every step you take, He takes two. He always shows up, even when we are in darkness. His Word, in 2 Corinthians 6:14, tells us that darkness cannot dwell where there is light. Show up, whatever your state, and the light of Jesus will push back the darkness on your behalf.

Study Scripture
Ephesians 6:10–18—The Armor of God

> 10 Finally, be strong in the Lord and in his mighty power. 11 Put on the full armor of God, so that you can take your stand against the devil's schemes. 12 For our struggle is not against flesh and blood, but against the rulers, against the authorities, against the powers of this dark world and against the spiritual forces of evil in the heavenly realms. 13 Therefore put on the full armor of God, so that when the day of evil comes, you may be able to stand your ground, and after you have done everything, to stand. 14 Stand firm then, with the belt of truth buckled around your waist, with the breastplate of righteousness in place, 15 and with your feet fitted with the readiness that comes from the gospel of peace. 16 In addition to all this, take up the shield of faith, with which you can extinguish all the flaming arrows of the evil one. 17 Take the helmet of salvation and the sword of the Spirit, which is the word of God.
>
> 18 And pray in the Spirit on all occasions with all kinds of prayers and requests. With this in mind, be alert and always keep on praying for all the Lord's people.

It matters how you dress when you show up. You don't bring a knife to a gun fight, wear flip flops when you're going hiking, or wear combat boots to a beach vacation. You have to be dressed for war, putting on the whole armor of God. I do not have time to go into an in-depth study on Ephesians 6, but that is something you should put on your CaveTime to-do list. Bottom line is that you must be ready for your enemy, prepared to push back the darkness. Read Ephesians 6 and pray it over your life and your family. As we talk about showing up, be dressed to kill!

Stone One: Show Up

As we discussed before, the number one tool of the enemy is to keep you out of the game. If you are not in the game, you cannot influence its outcome. I think most men (people) don't show up because they have a fear of failing. We don't want to strike out. What if I pray for that person and they are not healed? What if I say the wrong thing? What if I don't know what to say? What if I make a fool out of myself?

These fears are all based on you performing. On you delivering. On you having the answers. On you. On you. On you. That is such a lie of the enemy to keep you from showing up. It is really quite simple. As Pastor Rick Warren says in the first line of his book *Purpose Driven Life*, "It is not about you."[2]

It is about obedience. It is about trusting Him enough that you believe He will show up. It is about wanting to please Him so much that your fear of failing is faint compared to your desire to be counted on. Your mindset needs to be this: if God comes looking for someone, your answer is, "Here am I, Lord. Send me!"

Self vs. Others

Our human nature seems to rule over our actions more than our spirit nature does. Human nature tell us to put our hand down if we don't know the answer. That is the best example I can think of when it comes to our hesitance of showing up. We are fearful that we won't have the answer, that we might not get it right, that the person might not be receptive to us or our intervention. Human nature tell us it is better to just play it safe and not intervene. The less we know the person or circumstances, the more this holds true.

I am a CliffsNotes (my kids now tell me it is SparkNotes) kind of guy, so I'll just give you the bottom line. Showing up can be broken down to the following two simple points:

1. Replace any selfishness or fear of failure with thinking of others.

2. Replace your trust in your human knowledge with your trust in the Holy Spirit.

And that's all it is.

If I don't want to take the time to show up for my wife or spend time with my kids to really know what they are feeling or what struggles they are having, it only comes down to two reasons. I'd rather be doing something else that benefits me more like watching a ball game or doing office work, or it's plain and simple laziness. We don't think the effort to engage is worth the time. Let the wife do it. Let the youth pastor or their friends do it. We would rather do something that feeds our needs. Why cook dinner for the family when I have been working all day? I did my part by putting in a good eight to ten long hours, so I deserve to kick it back and be a couch potato. Sometimes that is cool, but I (and you) need to step up the plate and go to bat for those that put up with our crap (it's my book so I can say what I want) most of the time. If we are going to be honest, our spouses put in as much time as we do into their work and family.

My wife's love language is acts of service. If you don't know what the five love languages are, go get the book *The 5 Love Languages* by Gary Chapman. It will give great insight into your own needs as well as your family's. If I take the time to help clean the house or cook dinner while she is at work, she really feels loved and cared for. That is showing up. Believe me, the spiritual satisfaction is well worth the effort. (Yes, there can also be physical benefits for us married folk, but that is not supposed to be the sole reason.)

Take time to help someone who needs directions even if you are in a mad dash to get somewhere. I find myself not wanting to take the time to do something like that unless I can personally benefit from the time I put in. SELF-ISH-NESS. Do something for someone that has no return benefit. You might help the pastor trim the trees that fell in the storm, but what about the cranky old lady down the block who no one likes to talk to? If I help the pastor, I get some type of spiritual brownie points that I can cash in if I get caught or need to go fishing instead of helping set up the children's carnival. To help the old lady will be nothing but a headache. She'll neither like the job I did nor pay for anything. Thoughts to ponder, right?

I find that many of the times I don't choose to show up it's because, well, I just don't want to, which comes down to selfishness. I can give good excuses like I am really busy, I did something good last week, or it's somebody else's turn. Really? I wonder how we would feel if every time we needed God's grace, forgiveness or answers, He gave us some of the same lame excuses we give Him.

Bottom line: go the extra mile. Do more than what is required, and the blessings of Show Up will start to multiply in your life. Big show ups and small show ups are all a part of God's plan. Listen to the Holy Spirit prompting you to do something. Be what you are looking for. Be a blessing to receive your blessing. I promise you when you are showing up, you will start getting juiced and looking for the next opportunity.

Don't let Showtime be a channel on your cable (get rid of it if you have it). Let it be your new nickname. Jeff "SHOWtime" Voth at your service, Lord. I kinda feel like a superhero when I say that. What would happen to our families, our workplaces, our neighborhoods, our cities, and our country if all the men of God became SHOWtime superheroes? When God had something to be done…a kind word for someone…when any of his children needed to know that they were loved, that they were not a mistake, that they had purpose and destiny. All He would have to do when He needed to SHOW His love, would be to get on the super phone and get one of His SHOWtime men to go take care of business. I tell you what would happen. The Kingdom of God and His glory would permeate all darkness in the whole world. Let the S on your t-shirt stand for SHOWtime. Let the war cry for next session's Sling Time be: "Here am I, Lord. Send me!"

Human vs. Spirit

The second reason we don't show up is we are fearful that what we have is not good enough. We are not selfish, we just don't trust God enough to show up. Why would I go pray for the man who has cancer and has been sent home to die? I don't know what to say to him. He has never been to church and won't understand my Christianese. How can I pray for His healing when he is almost already dead? What if God does not heal him? Why put myself out there for that? What difference would it make? I'll just pray for Him in my quiet time, and it will count the same. Really? We don't trust God. We men are wired to have the answers, and if we don't, we fake it until we get out of the situation. Wear the mask. Keep it between the lines, play it safe, and all will be cool. We want to be William Wallace and face down injustice while standing against all the odds. It looks great in the movies, but no one really wants to put their head on the block for the simple chance to yell freedom right before their head is severed from their body.

Listen to what I am about to say. Don't miss this point. God holds you accountable for obeying, not for the end results. Whether the man gets healed or not is not up to you. It is up to God. If someone doesn't receive the word of encouragement you felt led to give. If the cranky little old lady down the street doesn't appreciate you taking your time and cleaning up the limbs in her yard. If the lady who takes your change on the toll road doesn't return your thank you.

It is okay. Do what God called you to do. Show up. Obey. We are so geared to get a favorable response that if we don't, we quit. I am not going to show up if he or she doesn't appreciate my effort. Really? How about we not worry about their responses or pats on the back and just worry about showing up.

Let's care more about what HE thinks, that our Lord and Savior can count on us to be obedient. Let's learn to be His go-to men no matter what the task. If it is a simple word of encouragement to the person behind the counter or serving someone of prestige, He can count on us. We are showing up on His behalf, for His purposes, to expand His kingdom. It is not about us, our ranking, or what we get. We are here to do His bidding.

So when we become men of the spirit and listen to our spirit man, we trust God to show up and do not worry about how we look, if we have the answers, or whether our task is received favorably. We look forward to stepping up to the plate not knowing exactly what we are going to say or do. We know that He, the One we serve, will give us the words to say or the action we should take. Now we are getting into some really cool territory. The gifts of the spirit that we read about in 1 Corinthians 12 come into play.

1 Corinthians 12 (The Message)—Spiritual Gifts

1–3 What I want to talk about now is the various ways God's Spirit gets worked into our lives. This is complex and often misunderstood, but I want you to be informed and knowledgeable. Remember how you were when you didn't know God, led from one phony god to another, never knowing what you were doing, just doing it because everybody else did it? It's different in this life. God wants us to use our intelligence, to seek to understand as well as we can. For instance, by using your heads, you know perfectly well that the Spirit of God would never prompt anyone to say "Jesus be damned!" Nor would anyone be inclined to say "Jesus is Master!" without the insight of the Holy Spirit.

4–11 *God's various gifts are handed out everywhere; but they all originate in God's Spirit. God's various ministries are carried out everywhere; but they all originate in God's Spirit. God's various expressions of power are in action everywhere; but God himself is behind it all. Each person is given something to do that shows who God is: Everyone gets in on it, everyone benefits. All kinds of things are handed out by the Spirit, and to all kinds of people! The variety is wonderful:*

wise counsel
clear understanding
simple trust
healing the sick
miraculous acts
proclamation
distinguishing between spirits
tongues
interpretation of tongues

All these gifts have a common origin, but are handed out one by one by the one Spirit of God. He decides who gets what, and when.

12–13 *You can easily enough see how this kind of thing works by looking no further than your own body. Your body has many parts—limbs, organs, cells—but no matter how many parts you can name, you're still one body. It's exactly the same with Christ. By means of his one Spirit, we all said good-bye to our partial and piecemeal lives. We each used to independently call our own shots, but then we entered into a large and integrated life in which he has the final say in every-thing. (This is what we proclaimed in word and action when we were baptized.) Each of us is now a part of his resurrection body, refreshed and sustained at one fountain—his Spirit—where we all come to drink. The old labels we once used to identify ourselves—labels like Jew or Greek, slave or free—are no longer useful. We need some-thing larger, more comprehensive.*

I am thoroughly convinced that the main reason we don't see more of the gifts of the spirit in action is we want them in operation *before* we show up. How about we trust God enough to show up with the gifts in tow after we choose to show up. Not before. I love verses 12–13 of The Message Bible: *We each used to independently call our own shots, but then we entered into a large and integrated life in which he has the final say in everything.* I really have gotten to that point in my life and am ashamed that it took me so long. I actually prefer to not know what I am going to do beforehand. I am less likely to get in the way. Showing up and operating as a conduit for the Holy Spirit in action is about not trusting yourself but trusting Him to do the work through you.

We are not all going to be speakers or orators, musicians, or master carpenters. We all have different talents, but we all can operate in the gifts by showing up. Sometimes it will use our talent, sometimes it will not. Don't fall into the trap that you can only show up in areas that you talented in. Wrong, dude! If we start doing that, then the preacher starts thinking it is beneath him to help the cranky old lady, and the master carpenter does not want to deliver a word of encouragement to the youth pastor. Bottom line, learn to let the Holy Spirit lead you. Look for opportunities to show up that are not preplanned. Let them be ordained. I call them divine connections or encounters. Just think how you feel when a comrade comes to you with a word of encouragement just when you need it most. We all like to receive. Let's be just as pumped to give.

Stone in Fright

Just so you know, when you start stepping out and showing up, you will not be perfect. I am a pastor and travel around the country almost every week speaking to men about CaveTime. I did not step into the pulpit my first time and hit it out of the park. I have actually gone back and listened to some of my first sermons and some were quite honestly painful. It takes practice to make perfect. I am sure my oratory skills have improved with time, but I also know that my ability to trust the Holy Spirit to show up and move on the hearts of men and women is what is really important. I pray that even when I failed in my presentation early on in my sermons as a pastor, the Holy Spirit still showed up and ministered to those in the congregation. I pray my trust in Him has grown to the level that I know no matter what I say or do, He is faithful to His Word and honors my effort.

It took me eight years to finally get the CaveTime message into book form. I am so glad I didn't write the book in those first few years. It took living in the cave all those years to perfect what God was saying to me and how I could convey it to you. Our CaveTime events look quite different than the very first one I did. God is still refining me and CaveTime. However, if I had never stepped out and been willing to fail, there would not be any CaveTime events. I trust God that no matter what, He will show up and touch the hearts of His people. He will use me if I make myself available. I pray each event gets better than the last. I get up every morning looking forward to the new revelations He will show me that I have never seen before. I embrace the failures, clumsy attempts at ministry, and meager beginnings and have made them the bricks that, put with the mortar of God's faithfulness, have built the wall that protects my family, friends, and you.

Stone in Flight

I want to give you an example of what the stone Show Up looks like in flight. How it turns from just a stone lying in a creek bed to a deadly weapon being hurled toward its mark from a sling. There is a man in my church named Doby. I know a little about his past. For the most part, his dad never really showed up for him as a kid. He is a builder and is quite successful. Instead of repeating what he experienced as a child, he is Mr. Show Up. He is always the first to put himself on the line. He is what I call a foxhole kind of guy. He is the one you want in your foxhole when the bullets start flying. He has your back, jack. He is also a guy you want to be with when the hunger pangs start. He knows every nook and cranny in a four-state area when it comes to good barbeque. He knows how to show up for barbeque and show up for those in his cave.

Once while eating barbeque at a little joint, he walked by some kids sitting in the dirt behind the building. He talked to some of the people standing there and found out that a small local church had opened their food pantry to the local families that needed help. The kids that were there playing in the dirt were waiting on their parents to get food. The only place to play was in the back of the building on a little bare spot of dirt where grass should have been. Doby didn't have much of a childhood and had to grow into a man much earlier than a young boy should have to. Doby decided right then and there that those kids needed a playground. Every child deserves to play. He found the pastor and told him he would be back in a couple of weeks with some of his crew to build them a playground. Doby was showing up. He did not know the pastor or any of the families or kids. He just felt compelled to show up and build them a playground. A trip to eat barbeque turned into a commitment to build a playground for some little kids whose situation probably could have been very similar to Doby's as a child.

Doby doesn't even know that I know that story. I don't know if the pastor ever thanked him or not. For the next several weeks, Doby spent time, both weekdays and weekends, building a playground for those kids. If you know Doby, he does nothing half-baked (didn't think I should use the other word). He built them a playground better than the one we have at church for our kids. He paid his guys to be on that job when they could have been on a project that made him money. Doby grew up with mostly leftovers, never getting the best of anything. His philosophy now is to give his best in everything. Show up and make it happen. Today some little kids are playing on a kickin' playground with a turbo slide while their parents (or single parent) stand in line for food. They get to feel like they matter, at least for that moment, because Doby decided to show up.

Doby has every reason not to show up in the natural. Most of his friends don't know what he went through as a child and even as a grown man. As an adult, he held his five-year-old son and watched him pass away from this life with a rare disease. He fought for the life of his wife who was given no chance to live with Stage IV cancer. Instead of using the pain of life as a reason to stay on the sidelines, Doby uses it for energy to show up. His child is in heaven, but he is taking care of those he doesn't even know or who can never repay him. That is Show Up in flight!

Are you ready to show up? Let's put the stone in our sling and use next session to let it fly. I hear the swooshing of slings all over the country spinning over the heads of superheroes! It's SHOWtime!

CAVE THREE

SLING TIME: SHOW UP

This is the Sling Cave. We learned about the principles and precepts of the Show Up stone. Hopefully you got stoked into placing the stone in your sling and getting it ready to fly. This cave session is all about slinging. Show Up in action. I have done my part in giving you what I know about the stone Show Up. This time is all about you doing it. All of your Show Up stones will not meet their marks. The point is that when you do it, you will get better. I want you to show up every day for the rest of your life.

This is where you become the writer. In this cave you are the one who fills these pages with the hieroglyphics of your CaveTime. These tell your story of using the stone to show up. The pictures and words are yours. Don't go to the next stone without putting this stone into practice. It is the foundation of all the other stones. You don't have to build a playground during this cave. You just have to start showing up by looking for opportunities. We are the hands and feet that Christ uses to touch the pains of the world.

Group Note

If you are doing this book as a group or FireTeam, use the time together to share your experiences—good and bad, happy and sad—during Sling Cave.

Spouse or significant other

_____

_____

_____

_____

_____

_____

_____

_____

_____

_____

_____

_____

_____

_____

Child or sibling

_____

_____

_____

_____

_____

_____

_____

_____

_____

_____

_____

_____

_____

_____

_____

CaveTime brother

_____

_____

_____

_____

_____

_____

_____

_____

_____

_____

_____

_____

_____

_____

Co-worker

_____

_____

_____

_____

_____

_____

_____

_____

_____

_____

_____

_____

_____

_____

Someone in the world

_____

_____

_____

_____

_____

_____

_____

_____

_____

_____

_____

_____

_____

_____

_____

_____

_____

Defeats of Sling Cave

Victories of Sling Cave

_____

_____

_____

_____

_____

_____

_____

_____

_____

_____

_____

_____

_____

_____

_____

_____

Practices to make this stone a part of my life

_____

_____

_____

_____

_____

_____

_____

_____

_____

_____

_____

_____

_____

_____

_____

_____

Other thoughts or scriptures

_____

_____

_____

_____

_____

_____

_____

_____

_____

_____

_____

_____

_____

_____

_____

WORSHIP

❝King David, although a man after God's own heart, was no stranger to shame. He had gone from Fearless Warrior to Fleeing Outcast. But during this time, he wrote:

> *"I sought the Lord and He answered me.*
> *He delivered me from all my fears.*
> *Those who look to Him are radiant.*
> *Their faces are never covered with shame."*
> *(Psalm 34:4–5)*

David knew he could declare war on his shame by worshipping the God that knew what to do with it. He realized the power of worship and how it caused him to focus on God and see His true greatness. One good look and David's perceived shame was ruled insignificant.

To worship in the face of darkness. To raise your voice and make a noise of honor unto your God. In the midst of pain, strife, or death, our God is strong and just. It takes some strength to worship our God in our darkest moments, but we worship. For He is worthy of our praise.**❞**

CAVE FOUR

STONE TIME: WORSHIP

Group Note

Show the video clip of the Worship stone. Have everyone read the following principles and discuss their thoughts and challenges. Discuss which areas you need to focus on in Sling Time for the stone.

Stone Two is Worship. There is a rhythm to the order of stones, and that is why Show Up is first. All of the stones build on each other, and if you don't show up, you can't do any of them. Worship naturally follows as the second stone. I hear from many of my cave-dwelling cohorts that the Worship stone is the hardest for them to do. I truly think this is due to our misconception of what worship is. We naturally think of worship as something we do at church before we listen to what the preacher has to say. We might on occasion participate in worship in a life group or small group setting if there is someone there who knows how to play the piano or guitar. That is a form of worship but not the definition of worship. Our human limitations on what we feel worship is can cause a huge mental block for many men. Let's start by defining what worship is.

Merriam-Webster defines worship as:

> **wor·ship**: the act of showing respect and love for a god especially by praying with other people who believe in the same god : the act of worshipping God or a god
>
> : excessive admiration for someone

Full Definition of *WORSHIP*

2: reverence offered a divine being or supernatural power; *also* : an act of expressing such reverence

3: a form of religious practice with its creed and ritual

4: extravagant respect or admiration for or devotion to an object or person.

I love the following words they use: the act of showing respect and love or excessive admiration for someone or an extravagant respect. These are powerful words that give us insight into what the stone of Worship should look like for us. Worship is the mindset in which we approach every aspect of our lives. It is not just something we do—it needs to be who we are. It is impossible to please God without worshipping him. It is the only reason we were created. It is the form of communication established to open all avenues and understanding of who God is. To worship is to be in God's presence, regardless of where we are, what we have done, or how we feel. I like to say it is turning your face toward God. No matter what has turned your head, you turn your face from it, back to the face of your Creator. If you are not in God's presence, if you do not have the ability to commune with Him, you are lost. I don't mean 'on the wrong street' lost. I am talking about 'on the wrong planet' lost. Worship is the most feared stone. But the stones of Worship build the bridge that spans the gap from sin and leads us back to the throne of our heavenly Father.

Dressed to Kill—War Zone

Nothing brings home the importance of worship like understanding the role the enemy of your soul held in heaven. Satan, the Devil, was at one time the heavenly leader in the area of worship. He was called Lucifer, which means "star of the day" or "son of the morning." He was an angel, but his role was different. He was considered to be an archangel. Ezekiel, an Old Testament prophet, gives us a good description of what Lucifer looked like when he thrived in his role as the leader of heavenly worship. Ezekiel 28: 11–14 (The Message) describes Satan.

> *"You had everything going for you.*
>> *You were in Eden, God's garden.*
> *You were dressed in splendor,*
>> *your robe studded with jewels:*
> *Carnelian, peridot, and moonstone,*
>> *beryl, onyx, and jasper,*
> *Sapphire, turquoise, and emerald,*
>> *all in settings of engraved gold.*
> *A robe was prepared for you*
>> *the same day you were created.*
> *You were the anointed cherub.*
>> *I placed you on the mountain of God.*
> *You strolled in magnificence*
>> *among the stones of fire.*
> *From the day of your creation*
>> *you were sheer perfection . . .*
>> *and then imperfection—evil!—was detected in you.*
> *In much buying and selling*
>> *you turned violent, you sinned!*
> *I threw you, disgraced, off the mountain of God.*
>> *I threw you out—you, the anointed angel-cherub.*
>> *No more strolling among the gems of fire for you!*
> *Your beauty went to your head.*
>> *You corrupted wisdom*
>> *by using it to get worldly fame.*
> *I threw you to the ground,*
>> *sent you sprawling before an audience of kings*
>> *and let them gloat over your demise.*

By sin after sin after sin,
*   by your corrupt ways of doing business,*
*   you defiled your holy places of worship.*
So I set a fire around and within you.
*   It burned you up. I reduced you to ashes.*
All anyone sees now
*   when they look for you is ashes,*
*   a pitiful mound of ashes.*
All who once knew you
*   now throw up their hands:*
'This can't have happened!
*   This* **has** *happened!'"*

Lucifer had everything. He was above all his peers in wisdom, beauty, and knowledge. He held the keys in his hand to enter into the presence of God Himself. What else could a guy want? He understood the ways of God and was the entrance to His presence. For Lucifer it was not enough. He wanted more. He wanted to be where God was...on the throne. He threw away probably the greatest job ever because he felt there was one more rung on the ladder he wanted to climb. He chose pride over worship. Flesh over spirit. He did not want to worship the God of all creation; he wanted to be the god of all. His archangel position was that of "covering." He was the head dude over covering and worship. Now are you getting where I'm going? Worship is covering. Isaiah 14 shows us the fall of Lucifer from the realm of heaven to the pits of hell.

Isaiah 14: 11–17 (The Message)

[11] This is where your pomp and fine music led you, Babylon,
*   to your underworld private chambers,*
A king-size mattress of maggots for repose
*   and a quilt of crawling worms for warmth.*

¹²What a comedown this, O Babylon!
   Daystar! Son of Dawn!
Flat on your face in the underworld mud,
   you, famous for flattening nations!

¹³⁻¹⁴You said to yourself,
   "I'll climb to heaven.
I'll set my throne
   over the stars of God.
I'll run the assembly of angels
   that meets on sacred Mount Zaphon.
I'll climb to the top of the clouds.
   I'll take over as King of the Universe!"

¹⁵⁻¹⁷But you didn't make it, did you?
   Instead of climbing up, you came down—
Down with the underground dead,
   down to the abyss of the Pit.

Who would understand the power of worship more than the one who was created from the beginning of time to lead it? Satan is the enemy of your soul and knows that if he can keep you from worship, he can keep you from the presence of God. Remove the covering, and you've got a target on your back and a sign on your forehead that says "IDIOT." Satan knows this. If he can get you to think it is all about you and your abilities, then he gets you to start moving away from the throne of God. Soon your face is turned towards those things that replace Him: idols. We, like Lucifer, start building little idols to ourselves, paying homage to how great we are. These are not always on purpose or blatant. Our house, our car, our trophy wife, our title at work…in and of themselves, they are not bad. It is when we wear them as our identity, as something we created, that we fall into pridefulness.

Pride turns into self-glorification (yeah, I made that word up) and then sin. I am not talking about the pride that we take in our work, as in being proud of our toil. I am talking about sharing the glory that is due Him. When Lucifer tried to take credit or glory of worship and put the light on his face instead of God's, he was removed from His presence. Unlike Satan, we realize our mistake, and shame keeps us hidden like Adam from the face of God. His shame of disobedience caused him to hide in the very place that was created for him to dwell: the Garden of Eden. What was created to be his sanctuary became his prison due to shame. Glory in who we are, our knowledge, or what we bring to the table always leads to sin. My dad always said, "Don't let your mouth write a check that your butt can't cash." What can you back up? We are nothing without Him. We were created for the sole purpose of communing with our Creator. Selfish pride leads us to believe we don't need God, and we end up removed from His presence.

That is why our relationship with Jesus Christ is so important. He is the Bright and Morning Star. He took the place that was vacated by Lucifer and now gives us access to dwell in the presence of Almighty God. He is seated at the right hand of Father God and serves as His Son.

Romans 8:34

> [34]Who then is the one who condemns? No one. Christ Jesus who died—more than that, who was raised to life—is at the right hand of God and is also interceding for us.

Satan, the enemy of your soul, does not want you to be covered. He was replaced with an advocate: Jesus Christ who is your covering. Don't let Satan rob you of your ability to worship. Your covering depends on it.

Study Scripture
Psalm 34

Of David. When he pretended to be insane before Abimelek, who drove him away, and he left.

¹I will extol the LORD at all times;

his praise will always be on my lips.

²I will glory in the LORD;

let the afflicted hear and rejoice.

³Glorify the LORD with me;

let us exalt his name together.

⁴I sought the LORD, and he answered me;

he delivered me from all my fears.

⁵Those who look to him are radiant;

their faces are never covered with shame.

⁶This poor man called, and the LORD heard him;

he saved him out of all his troubles.

⁷The angel of the LORD encamps around those who fear him,

and he delivers them.

⁸Taste and see that the LORD is good;

blessed is the one who takes refuge in him.

⁹Fear the LORD, you his holy people,

for those who fear him lack nothing.

¹⁰The lions may grow weak and hungry,

but those who seek the LORD lack no good thing.

¹¹Come, my children, listen to me;

I will teach you the fear of the LORD.

¹²Whoever of you loves life

and desires to see many good days,

¹³*keep your tongue from evil*
  and your lips from telling lies.
¹⁴*Turn from evil and do good;*
  seek peace and pursue it.
¹⁵*The eyes of the LORD are on the righteous,*
  and his ears are attentive to their cry;
¹⁶*but the face of the LORD is against those who do evil,*
  to blot out their name from the earth.

¹⁷*The righteous cry out, and the LORD hears them;*
  he delivers them from all their troubles.
¹⁸*The LORD is close to the brokenhearted*
  and saves those who are crushed in spirit.

¹⁹*The righteous person may have many troubles,*
  but the LORD delivers him from them all;
²⁰*he protects all his bones,*
  not one of them will be broken.

²¹*Evil will slay the wicked;*
  the foes of the righteous will be condemned.
²²*The LORD will rescue his servants;*
  no one who takes refuge in him will be condemned.

David knew what it was like to be removed from God's presence. He also knew what removed him from God: self which became sin. The great truth in this scripture is that David also knew that in all things, he needed to worship his Lord. He needed to turn his face toward the face of God. In all things (good or bad), at all times (happy or sad), and even in his darkness. David wrote this psalm when he was on the run from Saul who, by the way, he used to lead in worship. Saul was seeking his life, so he went to the camp of his enemy, the

Philistine king, and was lying out of his teeth while pretending to be crazy in order to save his hide. He was as far as he could be from his given position.

Even in that state, he recognized the reach of his Lord to find him and comfort him. He was hiding, lying, and cowering in a cave, yet he knew the power of worship. Even in that state, he chose to reach out to God in worship. He had lost his covering and, through worship, was trading his shame for the presence of God. In this cave as we learn about the stone of Worship, read this scripture one verse at a time and let it sink in. As you read it, replace David with yourself and his sin with your sin. Listen to this: **Worship is not about your worthiness. It is about His worthiness to receive it.** Worship Him because He is worthy of it! Turn your face toward Him and raise your masculine voice to praise the One who is worthy of all. There is a direct correlation with David's exploits as a warrior and his exploits as a worshipper. Let the same be said of you.

Stone Two: Worship

Worship is your covering. Even if you have removed yourself from His presence, you must worship to open the door. You have to turn your face back toward Him. Face your Creator. You understand now that it is not just the twenty minutes we spend before a sermon at church. Worship is the attitude in which you do everything. If you believe that He made you in His image, then you realize that everything you were created to be is based on glorifying Him. Maybe worship is so hard for us because no one knows us better than ourselves. We know our dirt, filth, and all the little things that make us imperfect. Those things that we are ashamed of. "Yeah Jeff, but you don't know what I did." Really? Pull off your mask and get real. We all have been there, covered in shame. We must remove the covering of shame that the enemy of our soul places on us and replace it with the covering of worship. Turn your face from the T&A on your computer and back to the face of God. Turn your face from the deep darkness of being separated from your God to the light of His wonderful face.

Masculine Voice

Some of us do this better than others. I take great comfort in raising my voice to my heavenly Father. I think it is because I, as a pastor, understand the power of setting the atmosphere of our time with God with the power of praise and worship. At church, people come in carrying the heaviness of the day, failures, pains, sorrows, anxiety, and all the weights of the week. We join together, begin to worship with our voices, and slowly but surely, the weights that bind and hinder our closeness to God begin to fall away. They become smaller and dimmer in the light of His glorious face. The carnal or flesh becomes weaker, and the essence of who we really are, our spirit man, becomes alive, regenerated, and full of our communion with Abba Father.

I love the CaveTime events where we as men come boldly to the foot of the cross and lay down the weights that we have been carrying. Shame, sorrow, discontent, regret, failures, anxiety, hidden secrets, and all of the junk that shackles us from the freedom His presence brings. Slowly the weeping of coarse male voices letting go of the chains that bind them turns into reverberating praise to the One that set them free. As the power of community fills the room, hundreds of voices become one strong force, pushing the darkness away from all who hear it as they turn their faces of shame toward their Master. Worship fills the room as men lay prostrate before their Maker, giving due to their Savior. Their praise becomes their covering as they set the tone for what God is going to do throughout the event.

Your voice is a form of worship that you need to learn to use. I am an early riser and go to my cave way before the rest of my family begins to stir. I put praise and worship music on and let it set the tone for my time with my King and permeate both the atmosphere and my spirit. I often begin to sing along and feel my spirit rise. As you practice your CaveTime, raise your voice to the One worthy of your praise. I make up my own words many times, singing my thoughts and prayers in the privacy of my cave. If during the day I am driving, I often sing the words of my heart as I pour out my soul to the One who made it. Whatever time works for you, worship Him in spirit and truth with your masculine voice. Let your voice of worship cover your life and your household.

All I Do

I believe that all we do can be—and should be—an act of worship. Even the most mundane tasks should be an act of worship. **Attitude determines your altitude**. Did you get that? I am sure you have heard it before, but we all need to hear it again. **Attitude determines your altitude.** The spirit in which you do something determines how much you enjoy it. You should do it as unto the Lord. Read what Colossians says.

Colossians 3:23–24

> *23Whatever you do, work at it with all your heart, as working for the Lord, not for human masters, 24since you know that you will receive an inheritance from the Lord as a reward. It is the Lord Christ you are serving.*

I love the way it reads in The Message Bible.

Colossians 3:23–25 (The Message)

> *22–25Servants, do what you're told by your earthly masters. And don't just do the minimum that will get you by. Do your best. Work from the heart for your real Master, for God, confident that you'll get paid in full when you come into your inheritance. Keep in mind always that the ultimate Master you're serving is Christ. The sullen servant who does shoddy work will be held responsible. Being a follower of Jesus doesn't cover up bad work.*

David understood the power of this as we have already read in Psalms 34. He starts out by stating, "*¹I will extol the LORD at all times; his praise will always be on my lips.*"

Really? At all times? In everything? I never said it would be easy. Don't think it is not a struggle for this old mountain boy from Colorado. I miss great opportunities each and every day. But it does not change the fact that I should. Or the power it has. If I can clean the toilet for the wife, run and get coffee for coworkers, choose the least pleasant task on Saturday workday at the church, and see it as unto the Lord, I am doing it as an act of worship. I am adding power and covering to my life. Try it. Remember, you are His representation to the world, His ambassador. Be a good one.

All I Say

How important is what I say?

Proverbs 18:21

> *²¹ The tongue has the power of life and death,*
> *   and those who love it will eat its fruit.*

The power of life and death? Come on, bro. Really? James thinks so.

James 3:6

> *⁶ The tongue also is a fire, a world of evil among the parts of the body.*
> *It corrupts the whole body, sets the whole course of one's life on fire,*
> *and is itself set on fire by hell.*

Death and Life. Now do you think what you say is powerful? God's Word has so much to say about the tongue of man. The greatest example of its power is in Romans.

Romans 10:9

> *⁹If you declare with your mouth, "Jesus is Lord," and believe in your heart that God raised him from the dead, you will be saved.*

So if the words of your mouth have the power to save you, don't you think they are important? If we treat the things that come out of our mouths as worship, I would hope they would be more uplifting and positive. I remember giving a ride home to one of my kids' friends from school. I did not know the girl, so I started asking her general questions about school, what she liked, etc. The girl must have said the words "I hate" fifty times in fifteen minutes. I really don't think she hated everything, but she soon will.

What if we taped every word that came out of our mouths for one day and played it back that evening? I wonder how often I would sound like the girl I gave a ride home to. Treat your words and thoughts as worship. You may not believe them at first, but they have the power to change your countenance and how you carry yourself. Try and use your words to bless your Lord. Let your words be a covering, not a cursing. Let them be worship.

Stone in Fright

I feel that men are afraid today, maybe now more than ever. They are afraid to be men. Afraid to stand. And certainly afraid to raise their masculine voices, especially in the name of their Lord Jesus, on behalf of the people for whom they have been called to stand as a wall. This is where worship starts. A man raising his voice to God...for God. And I am not just talking about singing in church. I am talking about a man's life being a masculine song in the world. The lines of what this means have become blurred. Society has blurred the lines so much that a man almost has to apologize for his masculinity. He is called to be more of a metrosexual which is a blending of genders into a softer, feministic role. Is it any wonder the world says it is okay for a boy to take his time to decide which gender he feels more akin too? With the loss of father figures in our society, many young men are being raised by mothers and grandmothers without the God-designed influence of males.

Scripture tells us that God created humans in His image, and within the context of that image, there are masculine and feminine roles. The image that God created is within each male, but as a result of humanity and sin, there has been a diabolical conspiracy through the ages to strip the male of that role and blur his recognition of what male looks like and how male acts.

Stone in Flight

I was part of an event recently that bolstered my hope in what God is doing in men in our nation, especially young ones. I had just finished speaking to a group of about 100 young men in a college retreat setting. My wife Lori had just finished with the women. We joined the groups for a final service where we were going to have communion, pray, and then go home…but something powerful happened. One of the young men stepped to a mic before I did and said, "Men, we need to raise our voices and sing over these women. We need to stand up, surround them, and sing over them." He then set the mic down and began singing the doxology. "Praise God from whom all blessings flow, praise Him all creatures here below. Praise Him above ye heavenly host. Praise Father, Son, and Holy Ghost. Amen." Women began to weep and then sob. They sobbed in safety. They sobbed because of safety. They felt what it was like to have a wall of men surround them and raise their masculine voices on their behalves. Many of the young ladies stated that they had never felt what they felt on that day. Women were made safe, and men were empowered. The raising of masculine voices to God on behalf of others brings the fight to the enemy in a powerful way.

CAVE FIVE

SLING TIME: WORSHIP

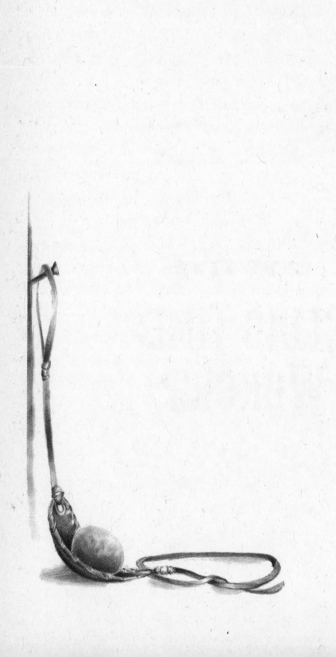

This is Sling Time. We learned about the principles and precepts of the Worship stone. Hopefully you got stoked into placing the stone in your sling and getting it ready to fly. This cave is all about slinging. Worship in action. Worshipping Him in all situations and with everything you do. I am sure you will listen to more worship music, and I happen to know of a good CD you can use. Set the atmosphere for worship. Let your whole life be an offering. I have done my part in giving you what I know about the stone Worship. Now it is your time to worship. This cave is all about doing. All of your Worship stones will not meet their marks. The point is when you do it, you will get better. I want everything you do to be an act of worship for the rest of your life.

This is where you become the writer. You are the one who fills these pages with the hieroglyphics of your CaveTime. These tell your story of using the stone of Worship. The pictures and words are yours. Don't go to the next stone without putting into practice this stone. It is the covering for all you do. You don't have to write a psalm or dance in the street like David did. You just have to start worshiping God in all things. Every situation is a chance, a challenge to worship. It will be your covering and will set the atmosphere and tone of your life.

Group Note

If you are doing this book as a group or FireTeam, use the time together to share your experiences—good and bad, happy and sad—during Sling Time.

What areas in your life are easy to worship or hard to worship in?

_____

_____

_____

_____

_____

_____

_____

_____

_____

_____

_____

_____

_____

_____

Did your worship remove your shame?

What areas are challenges for you to worship in?

_____

_____

_____

_____

_____

_____

_____

_____

_____

_____

_____

_____

_____

_____

_____

How did you worship by doing?

_____

_____

_____

_____

_____

_____

_____

_____

_____

_____

_____

_____

_____

_____

_____

How did you worship with your words?

_____

_____

_____

_____

_____

_____

_____

_____

_____

_____

_____

_____

_____

_____

Defeats of Sling Time

_____

_____

_____

_____

_____

_____

_____

_____

_____

_____

_____

_____

_____

_____

_____

Victories of Sling Time

_____

_____

_____

_____

_____

_____

_____

_____

_____

_____

_____

_____

_____

_____

_____

_____

Practices to make this stone a part of your life

Other thoughts or scriptures

_____

_____

_____

_____

_____

_____

_____

_____

_____

_____

_____

_____

_____

_____

_____

PRAYER

The righteous cry out, and the Lord hears them.
He delivers them from all their troubles.
(Psalm 34:17)

"David knew without hesitation that God would hear and deliver him from the assaults that were being leveled at him. He knew this because he had seen God protect him as he fought both the lion and the bear and then the giant. And he would also be delivered from the situation that had driven him to the cave.

It was second nature for David to talk with God conversationally, to tell Him what was on his heart and then listen and hear from God. David knew that God would move. He didn't necessarily know **how** God would move, but he knew that He would because of faithful, honest prayer.

Prayer is an opportunity to hear from God about how He wants us to speak, respond, and conduct ourselves through our masculinity. On His behalf. Showing Up sets the foundation between a man and God. Worship provides the focus: a man's face pointed toward God's face. And Prayer provides an avenue for those two faces to have a conversation."

CAVE SIX

STONE TIME: PRAYER

Group Note

Show the video clip of the Prayer stone. Have everyone read the following principles and discuss their thoughts and challenges. Discuss which areas you need to focus on in Sling Time for the stone.

Stone Three is Prayer. As we discussed before, there is a method to the order of the stones. We have to Show Up first before any of the stones can be practiced. We have to set the atmosphere of our covering by using the stone of Worship, and then once in the presence of God, we use the stone of Prayer to communicate to the One who made us. There have been more books written on prayer than maybe any other biblical subject, and with good reason. Prayer is our intimate communication with the Creator of the universe, our Maker.

Dressed to Kill—War Zone

In war, one of the first acts of winning is to cut off your enemy's lines of communication. If they are not able to coordinate their movements or get information from the front lines to headquarters, they cannot attack. Miscommunication or the lack of communication always leads to defeat. Yeah, you get it, don't you? You can bet the enemy of your soul gets it. If he can keep you from communicating with your God, there is no way you can fight the good fight or win in life. Prayer is our communication. Is it important? You betcha. How important? Let's just say it needs to be more than just something we do before we scarf down barbeque.

Prayer halts the advancement of the enemy. It is the stone you use to bind the darkness that threatens you and all you love. The words of Jesus explain this in Matthew 12.

Matthew 12:22–30 (The Message)—No Neutral Ground

22–23Next a poor demon-afflicted wretch, both blind and deaf, was set down before him. Jesus healed him, gave him his sight and hearing. The people who saw it were impressed—"This has to be the Son of David!"

24But the Pharisees, when they heard the report, were cynical. "Black magic," they said. "Some devil trick he's pulled from his sleeve."

25–27Jesus confronted their slander. "A judge who gives opposite verdicts on the same person cancels himself out; a family that's in a constant squabble disintegrates; if Satan banishes Satan, is there any Satan left? If you're slinging devil mud at me, calling me a devil kicking out devils, doesn't the same mud stick to your own exorcists?

28–29"But if it's by God's power that I am sending the evil spirits packing, then God's kingdom is here for sure. How in the world do you think it's possible in broad daylight to enter the house of an awake, able-bodied man and walk off with his possessions unless you tie him up first? Tie him up, though, and you can clean him out.

30"This is war, and there is no neutral ground. If you're not on my side, you're the enemy; if you're not helping, you're making things worse.

Yeah. That's right. Your prayers bind the strong man. I love how The Message Bible states it in verse 30: "This is war, and there is no neutral ground." Sounds like winner takes all to me.

Prayer is your source of power that the enemy wants to stop. No prayer, no power. Bottom line. It's pretty much that simple. To be dressed to kill, you have to be armed with the stone of Prayer.

Study Scripture
Matthew 7:7–12— Ask, Seek, Knock

7 "Ask and it will be given to you; seek and you will find; knock and the door will be opened to you. 8 For everyone who asks receives; the one who seeks finds; and to the one who knocks, the door will be opened.

9 "Which of you, if your son asks for bread, will give him a stone? 10 Or if he asks for a fish, will give him a snake? 11 If you, then, though you are evil, know how to give good gifts to your children, how much more will your Father in heaven give good gifts to those who ask him! 12 So in everything, do to others what you would have them do to you, for this sums up the Law and the Prophets.

2 Chronicles 7:14

14 if my people, who are called by my name, will humble themselves and pray and seek my face and turn from their wicked ways, then I will hear from heaven, and I will forgive their sin and will heal their land.

Hebrews 4:15–16

15 For we do not have a high priest who is unable to empathize with our weaknesses, but we have one who has been tempted in every way, just as we are—yet he did not sin. 16 Let us then approach God's throne of grace with confidence, so that we may receive mercy and find grace to help us in our time of need.

Mark 11:24

24 Therefore I tell you, whatever you ask for in prayer, believe that you have received it, and it will be yours.

John 14:13–14

> *13And I will do whatever you ask in my name, so that the Father may be glorified in the Son. 14You may ask me for anything in my name, and I will do it.*

James 5:16

> *16Therefore confess your sins to each other and pray for each other so that you may be healed. The prayer of a righteous person is powerful and effective.*

There are so many good passages from the Bible on prayer. I only picked a few. I think these give you an idea of how important the stone of Prayer is to have in your pouch. Prayer is an act of obedience that we are commanded to do numerous times in God's Word. When we pray, we are creating intimacy with our Father, obeying His commandments. It is not just out of obedience that God commands us to pray; it is for our benefit. Just as worship is often misunderstood by many men and therefore not practiced, I find prayer is handled the same way. How do I pray? When do I pray? Does God hear my prayers? Am I worthy of praying? Does it matter if I keep my eyes open? (Don't act like you have never asked that question.)

Ponder the scriptures above as we learn not only *why* we should pray, but *how* we should pray and *what* we should pray for. With the stone of Prayer, you will be powerful and effective.

Stone Three: Prayer

If worship is the light switch that gives you access to the light, prayer is the power that turns the lights on. Prayer is power. No prayer, no power. Simple but true. I have had times when my prayer life was lacking, and it showed. There have been times when I was dialed in tight with the stone of Prayer, and it showed. I feel it is the most transparent of the stones. You know whether it is being used or not. You can't fake it 'til you make it with prayer.

Spiritual Food

C.S. Lewis compares man's relationship with God to food in his classic piece *Mere Christianity.* "God designed the human machine to run on Himself. He Himself is the fuel our spirits were designed to burn, or the food our spirits were designed to feed on. There is no other."[3]

What a great analogy that especially applies to the stone of Prayer. I love to go up into the mountains of Colorado where I grew up. Even now that I live several states away, at least once each summer I grab my boys and some cave mates and head for the crystal, pristine, and raw beauty that only exists 10,000 feet above sea level. If you have ever flown into Denver, the first thing you notice is the lack of air. At one mile above sea level (over 5,000 feet), the air is thin, especially if your body has not acclimated to it. Backpack up into the mountains, toting everything you will need for a week, and your lungs and legs will burn like fire.

You have to be prepared to go up that high. In order to function properly, at least one month before I go each summer, I have to really start preparing my body through conditioning and especially with my diet. If I eat junk food for the month before I go, guess what? The mountains win, and I get my butt kicked. When I need the extra energy or stamina to climb from 5,000 feet to 10,000 feet, it is not there. I have to eat right. Lean and mean. Then when the circumstances of the mountains demand the energy to climb, pack, and suck the thin air, I have the ability to do so. (Though I will admit it's harder now than when I was wrestling in high school.) You get it now, don't you?

Prayer is the food your spiritual body needs to function and move forward in this life. Just as you need to consume the proper foods for your physical body to function properly, your spirit has to consume the proper spiritual food to live.

The most important things I have to have when I hike into the wilderness are water first, then food. Miscalculate either one of those, and a relaxing excursion into the woods turns into a fight for survival. Your spirit has no chance if it is starved for prayer. Remember it is the power that your spirit runs on. It is the fuel for your fire. Huge fuel, huge fire. Small fuel, small fire. No fuel, no fire. Life is tough enough as it is. Prayer gives us the capacity to not only survive, but to thrive. The more time I take to prepare to go into the mountains, the easier and more enjoyable the trip is. It is the same for our spirits and prayer. Lord, let us be men of prayer that we may cover, protect, and conquer in Your name.

Conversation

Prayer is conversation with God. Conversation is not just talking, it is listening. We share with our heavenly Father the burdens and joys of our heart and listen in our spirit man for His still, small voice. Brother Lawrence was a monk who lived a simple life almost entirely within the walls of a French monastery in the 1600s. His book *The Practice of the Presence of God* has been a go-to manual for great men of God like A.W. Tozer and John Wesley. Written over four hundred years ago, it serves as one of the greatest examples of how we should use the stones of Worship, Prayer, and Word. Brother Lawrence knew the power of conversing with God.

> "That we should establish ourselves in a sense of GOD's Presence,
> by continually conversing with Him. That it was a shameful thing to
> quit His conversation, to think of trifles and fooleries."[4]

He knew that prayer was not just him asking God for something. It was like talking to a father or dear friend. Intimacy with God comes through prayer, which is conversation, which means talking and listening.

I regard myself as the most wretched of all men, stinking and covered with sores, and as one who has committed all sorts of crimes against his King. Overcome by remorse, I confess all my wickedness to Him, ask His pardon and abandon myself entirely to Him to do with as He will. But this King, filled with goodness and mercy, far from chastising me, lovingly embraces me, makes me eat at His table, serves me with His own hands, gives me the keys of His treasures and treats me as His favorite. He talks with me and is delighted with me in a thousand and one ways; He forgives me and relieves me of my principle bad habits without talking about them; I beg Him to make me according to His heart and always the more weak and despicable I see myself to be, the more beloved I am of God.[5]

Brother Lawrence spent most of his time at the monastery, serving the other monks in the kitchen. He did not view his mundane task of scrubbing pots any differently than being on his knees in prayer.

The time of business does not with me differ from the time of prayer; and in the noise and clatter of my kitchen, while several persons are at the same time calling for different things, I possess God in as great tranquility as if I were upon my knees before the Blessed Sacrament.[6]

Continual Prayer

The time I spend on my knees cannot be replaced. I have to have that quiet time. But prayer is not just the time when you close your eyes and speak to God. Like worship, it is a continual mindset that you should be in throughout the day. Brother Lawrence saw what he did throughout the day as a time of prayer.

The sacredness or worldly status of a task mattered less than motivation behind it. "Nor is it needful that we should have great things to do...We can do little things for God; I turn the cake that is frying on the pan for love of him, and that done, if there is nothing else to call me, I prostrate myself in worship before him, who has given me grace to work; afterwards I rise happier than a king. It is enough for me to pick up but a straw from the ground for the love of God.[7]

What would happen if my daily work and play were part of my conversation with God? I tell you when you are in that zone, you feel the power. We should always be in what I call a mindset of prayer, just as if we were talking to our best friend or wife. You don't have to formalize the intimate time you have with your cave mates. It is natural. That is exactly what it should be with your prayer time with God. Natural, free, and sometimes without beginning or end. It is important to have that dedicated quiet time with the Lord on a daily basis. I am a morning guy, so my time is in the morning. It usually is a part of my CaveTime and sets up my day for power and success. All guys are not like that. I have cave mates that have their special time with God at night, after the cares of the day have waned and given up to the solace of the night. Find whatever time is right for you.

Prayer includes our quiet time and the times we kneel with our children by their beds, but it also encompasses all the hours and minutes of the day. Walk in an attitude of prayer that keeps your conversation with God ongoing. It might feel weird at first, but it will become more natural as you practice it. My prayer for you and me is that, like Brother Lawrence, we learn to practice the presence of God in all we do, using the stones of Worship and Prayer continually and in all things.

Prayer Is

I want to write a prayer manual that helps guys in their CaveTime really focus on the attributes and benefits of living a prayerful life. I don't have time to do that here, but I want to give you some quick biblical and foundational truths of what you can and should expect from the stone of Prayer. The more you use it, the better and more accurate you will be with it. Prayer will become a go-to stone that you reach for daily and place in your sling. Paul shows us in Philippians exactly how to pray.

Philippians 4:4–7

> *4Rejoice in the Lord always. I will say it again: Rejoice! 5Let your gentleness be evident to all. The Lord is near. 6Do not be anxious about anything, but in every situation, by prayer and petition, with thanksgiving, present your requests to God. 7And the peace of God, which transcends all understanding, will guard your hearts and your minds in Christ Jesus.*

Following are only a few of the attributes of prayer along with coinciding scriptures. As you learn to use the stone of Prayer, these will help you in designing your personal conversation with God.

Power: Matthew 26:41

> *41Watch and pray so that you will not fall into temptation. The spirit is willing, but the flesh is weak.*

Receive: Hebrews 4:15–16

¹⁵*For we do not have a high priest who is unable to empathize with our weaknesses, but we have one who has been tempted in every way, just as we are—yet he did not sin.* ¹⁶*Let us then approach God's throne of grace with confidence, so that we may receive mercy and find grace to help us in our time of need.*

Ask: John 14:13–14

¹³*And I will do whatever you ask in my name, so that the Father may be glorified in the Son.* ¹⁴*You may ask me for anything in my name, and I will do it.*

Confession: James 5:16

¹⁶*Therefore confess your sins to each other and pray for each other so that you may be healed. The prayer of a righteous person is powerful and effective.*

Intercession: Romans 8:26–27

²⁶*In the same way, the Spirit helps us in our weakness. We do not know what we ought to pray for, but the Spirit himself intercedes for us with groans that words cannot express.* ²⁷*And he who searches our hearts knows the mind of the Spirit, because the Spirit intercedes for the saints in accordance with God's will.*

Comfort: Psalms 23:4

⁴*Even though I walk through the darkest valley, I will fear no evil, for you are with me; your rod and your staff, they comfort me.*

Stone in Fright

Fear will grip and debilitate you. So much so that sometimes you can't even move. You hear voices. Some of them from the past and some from the future. Voices that confuse, taunt, and mock you. This has happened to me more times than I can count and often at night. I remember one time in particular I was in the middle of an unexpected job transition (meaning that I resigned from a job before I was fired), and I had no idea what I was going to do. Voices told me that I was an idiot for taking the job in the first place. That I was going to lose my house. They were almost deafening. My heart was racing, my mouth was dry, and I was at a loss for what to do. The moment of decision was upon me, and I could not make one. So...

Stone in Flight

...I called my best friend, and we had a conversation with each other and then with God. We talked about beating on some people (and how that might get us in real trouble). We talked about possible alternatives, and we talked about how God had never failed either one of us before. A brother talked me off a ledge and into a conversation with God. That conversation led to more with both him and my Father and ultimately a new job after some miraculous provision from the war room of Heaven. Conversation with a brother and our Father. We slung the stone of Prayer in the face of fear and taunting voices.

CAVE SEVEN

SLING TIME: PRAYER

This is Sling Time. We learned about the principles and precepts of the Prayer stone. I think by now you realize that in order to live a life of power, you have to live a life of prayer. You are now ready to put the stone of Prayer in your sling so it can start to zing. This cave is all about slinging. Prayer in flight. This cave is all about doing. All of your Prayer stones will not meet their marks. At times they might even feel clumsy. The point is when you do it, you will get better. This is where you become the writer.

In this cave you are the one who fills these pages with the hieroglyphics of your CaveTime. These tell your story of using the stone of Prayer. The pictures and words are yours. Don't go to the next stone without putting into practice this stone. It is the power for all you do. You don't have to have all of your prayer practices down. Learn to live a life where you are in constant conversation with God about all and in all. I want you to live a life of prayer so you become the strong man in your house, job, and family. Build a house of prayer!

Group Note

If you are doing this book as a group or FireTeam, use the time together to share your experiences—good and bad, happy and sad—during Sling Time.

How did you incorporate your quiet time?

How did you incorporate your daily routine into stones of Prayer?

_____

_____

_____

_____

_____

_____

_____

_____

_____

_____

_____

_____

_____

_____

_____

How was your prayer for **power**?

_____

_____

_____

_____

_____

_____

_____

_____

_____

_____

_____

_____

_____

_____

_____

What did you pray to **receive**?

_____

_____

_____

_____

_____

_____

_____

_____

_____

_____

_____

_____

_____

_____

What did you **ask** for in prayer?

Was it easy to **confess** in prayer?

_____

_____

_____

_____

_____

_____

_____

_____

_____

_____

_____

_____

_____

_____

_____

What did you **intercede** for in prayer?

_____

_____

_____

_____

_____

_____

_____

_____

_____

_____

_____

_____

_____

_____

_____

_____

Did you receive **comfort** in prayer?

_____

_____

_____

_____

_____

_____

_____

_____

_____

_____

_____

_____

_____

_____

_____

_____

Defeats of Sling Time

_____

_____

_____

_____

_____

_____

_____

_____

_____

_____

_____

_____

_____

_____

_____

Victories of Sling Time

_____

_____

_____

_____

_____

_____

_____

_____

_____

_____

_____

_____

_____

_____

_____

_____

Practices to make this a stone a part of my life

_____

_____

_____

_____

_____

_____

_____

_____

_____

_____

_____

_____

_____

_____

_____

Other thoughts or scriptures

_____

_____

_____

_____

_____

_____

_____

_____

_____

_____

_____

_____

_____

_____

WORD

As for God, his way is perfect.
The word of the Lord is flawless.
He is a shield for all who take refuge in Him.
For who is the rock except our God?
It is God who arms me with strength and makes my way perfect.
He makes my feet like the feet of a deer; he
enables me to stand on the heights.
He trains my hands for battle; my arms can bend a bow of bronze.
(Psalm 18:30–34)

"God spoke directly to King David and his mighty men in the cave, and in those words He shielded them. He armed them and instructed them how and where to go. David compared interaction with God to the practice of shooting a bow of bronze. With many repeated efforts, their strength and accuracy would begin to sharpen.

Interaction with the Word is no different. Through its repeated use, we develop its strength in us. The Word gave them the ability to get the all-important high ground in battle and the strength and strategic knowledge to strike at the appropriate instance. We develop the ability to interact with the Word **formationally**: to allow God's word to form us and change us into the men He wants us to be so that we might go into the world and stand as the **wall** that our people so desperately need.**"**

CAVE EIGHT

STONE TIME: WORD

Group Note

Show the video clip of the Word stone. Have everyone read the following principles and discuss their thoughts and challenges. Discuss which areas you need to focus on in Sling Time for the stone.

Stone Four is Word, as in God's Word with a capital W. Remembering that there is order in the stones, God's Word is the foundation that all the other stones are grounded in. If there was a large boulder that broke into rocks and tumbled down the mountain into the stream, the stones of Show Up, Worship, Prayer, and Community would have come from the rock of Word. All other stones find their source in the Word of God. God's Word is the foundation on which all other stones are built. If we were using the stones to build a wall, the Word stone would be on the bottom, laying a solid foundation for all the other stones to rest on. As we become a wall for each other and our families, the stone of Word is the support stone that all else rests on.

Dressed to Kill—War Zone

There has been a diabolical attempt to kill the Word of God since the beginning of time. Remember when Lucifer was cast out of heaven because of his pride and desire to build his own throne and kingdom? It continued at the dawn of humanity. In the garden, Satan asked Eve if God really meant that they couldn't eat from the tree.

Genesis 3:1

> [1] *Now the serpent was more crafty than any of the wild animals the LORD God had made. He said to the woman, "Did God really say, 'You must not eat from any tree in the garden'?"*

He wanted her to question the true meaning of what God said. Maybe He meant something different? Maybe she should interpret differently what He said? Maybe she needed to consider the circumstances, culture, and delivery of what He said? How could she be so sure of what Almighty God was trying to say? Who was she to say she knew what God meant? Isn't that kind of proud to say she knew what God knows? He is a God of love; surely He would not care if they ate from the tree of good and evil. Even if it was a little compromise, what difference would that make? Later in verse 13, Eve answers God when confronted: *"the serpent deceived me, and I ate of the tree."* Believe me bro, the serpent is still deceiving today with the question, *Did God really say*? (Maybe this is why I am not much of a snake guy.)

The same argument that occurred in the Garden of Eden continues today and, in my opinion, rages even hotter. The authenticity of God's Word was called into question in the garden, and the assault on Truth has never waned. What makes it even more confusing is that much of the onslaught is coming from inside the church as well as from secular culture. The goal is to dismantle, reinterpret, discount, rewrite, and neutralize its importance and the meaning of God's Word as absolute Truth. If God's Word is not accepting of my lifestyle, fleshly desires, and character, then let's redefine what it is. Disguised as tolerance, love, and acceptance, absolute Truth (capital T) is transformed into relative truth (little t) that is defined by culture, circumstances, and sin. Can't we all just get along, brother? HELL says no.

John 10:10

> *10 The thief comes only to steal and kill and destroy; I have come that they may have life, and have it to the full.*

Satan is still trying to kill. His mission was to kill the seed of Jesus then, and his current mission is to kill the seed of Christ in you. Everybody is okay and feeling the love until the name of Jesus comes in. Just don't use that name. The first church in Acts dealt with it, and so will you. Jesus lives in you, so guess what? You bet. The enemy's goal is to kill, maim, or render invalid the power of Jesus Christ in you. Turn off the switch of worship, cut the power of prayer, and eliminate the Word (the electric company that sends the juice down the line). The whole Bible from beginning to end warns and prepares us for this battle against the Word. Jesus says the world will hate you.

John 15:18–19

> *18 "If the world hates you, keep in mind that it hated me first. 19 If you belonged to the world, it would love you as its own. As it is, you do not belong to the world, but I have chosen you out of the world. That is why the world hates you."*

So much for the no-war culture. We are in the battle of the ages, where the kingdom of good and evil collide for winner takes all. We live on that cusp, my brothers. Our tools of combat are forged in the coals of Truth, God's Word. No weapon formed against you shall prosper. Men of valor, arm yourselves with the truth and light of God's Word and give not an inch to the god of this world in your families or lives. Stand firm.

Study Scripture
Psalms 119

The scripture of study for this cave is Psalms 119. It is the longest chapter in the Bible and contains 176 verses. This one chapter has more verses than fourteen Old Testament Books and seventeen New Testament books. Must be important, right? You bet, hoss. It is known in Hebrew by its opening words, *"Ashrei temimei derech"* which translate into *"happy are those whose way is perfect."* It is also known as the prayer for one who holds in high esteem and honors the sacred Hebrew law called Torah. The Torah is the written Word of God which we call the first five books of the Bible.

Listen to this. Almost every single verse in the whole chapter has a direct reference to the Word. The references of precepts, truth, promise, sacred law, commands, statues, your answers, decrees, and your words...all refer to God's Word. Dang important if you ask me. I would say the writer is trying to get a point across, don't you think?

Guess who wrote this Psalm? Technically it does not say, but most scholars and Hebrew rabbis concur that King David did. I think that's pretty cool. The guy who chose five stones to kill the giant wrote the description of how important the stone of the Word is. You can't make this stuff up, guys. Many feel that he wrote it in his later years when his locks of red had turned wisdom gray. In retrospection, as he took inventory of the victories and failures his life contained, he chose to pen the Psalm of Word as the single most important practice a wise man could follow.

It is written in an acrostic format, meaning that the first letters of each line follow through the Hebrew alphabet. The Orthodox Church and many tribes of Christian institutions hold that David wrote this Psalm as a way to teach his son Solomon the Hebrew alphabet. Not just the literary alphabet of the flesh for the task of writing and reading, but the alphabet of the spirit man for guidance and instruction. Can I get an amen from my brothers in the cave!

Let it be the same for you. Read, pray, and study the 119th Psalm not only for this cave, but all the days of your life. Build your house on the stone of Word. WORD UP my brothers, and let's kick some devil booty.

Psalm 119

Aleph
¹*Blessed are those whose ways are blameless,*
   who walk according to the law of the LORD.
²*Blessed are those who keep his statutes*
   and seek him with all their heart—
³*they do no wrong*
   but follow his ways.
⁴*You have laid down precepts*
   that are to be fully obeyed.
⁵*Oh, that my ways were steadfast*
   in obeying your decrees!
⁶*Then I would not be put to shame*
   when I consider all your commands.
⁷*I will praise you with an upright heart*
   as I learn your righteous laws.
⁸*I will obey your decrees;*
   do not utterly forsake me.

Beth
⁹*How can a young person stay on the path of purity?*
   By living according to your word.
¹⁰*I seek you with all my heart;*
   do not let me stray from your commands.
¹¹*I have hidden your word in my heart*
   that I might not sin against you.

¹²*Praise be to you, L*ORD*;*
teach me your decrees.
¹³*With my lips I recount*
all the laws that come from your mouth.
¹⁴*I rejoice in following your statutes*
as one rejoices in great riches.
¹⁵*I meditate on your precepts*
and consider your ways.
¹⁶*I delight in your decrees;*
I will not neglect your word.

Gimel
¹⁷*Be good to your servant while I live,*
that I may obey your word.
¹⁸*Open my eyes that I may see*
wonderful things in your law.
¹⁹*I am a stranger on earth;*
do not hide your commands from me.
²⁰*My soul is consumed with longing*
for your laws at all times.
²¹*You rebuke the arrogant, who are accursed,*
those who stray from your commands.
²²*Remove from me their scorn and contempt,*
for I keep your statutes.
²³*Though rulers sit together and slander me,*
your servant will meditate on your decrees.
²⁴*Your statutes are my delight;*
they are my counselors.

Daleth

25 I am laid low in the dust;

    preserve my life according to your word.

26 I gave an account of my ways and you answered me;

    teach me your decrees.

27 Cause me to understand the way of your precepts,

    that I may meditate on your wonderful deeds.

28 My soul is weary with sorrow;

    strengthen me according to your word.

29 Keep me from deceitful ways;

    be gracious to me and teach me your law.

30 I have chosen the way of faithfulness;

    I have set my heart on your laws.

31 I hold fast to your statutes, LORD;

    do not let me be put to shame.

32 I run in the path of your commands,

    for you have broadened my understanding.

He

33 Teach me, LORD, the way of your decrees,

    that I may follow it to the end.[b]

34 Give me understanding, so that I may keep your law

    and obey it with all my heart.

35 Direct me in the path of your commands,

    for there I find delight.

36 Turn my heart toward your statutes

    and not toward selfish gain.

37 Turn my eyes away from worthless things;

    preserve my life according to your word.[c]

³⁸Fulfill your promise to your servant,
   so that you may be feared.
³⁹Take away the disgrace I dread,
   for your laws are good.
⁴⁰How I long for your precepts!
   In your righteousness preserve my life.

Waw

⁴¹May your unfailing love come to me, LORD,
   your salvation, according to your promise;
⁴²then I can answer anyone who taunts me,
   for I trust in your word.
⁴³Never take your word of truth from my mouth,
   for I have put my hope in your laws.
⁴⁴I will always obey your law,
   for ever and ever.
⁴⁵I will walk about in freedom,
   for I have sought out your precepts.
⁴⁶I will speak of your statutes before kings
   and will not be put to shame,
⁴⁷for I delight in your commands
   because I love them.
⁴⁸I reach out for your commands, which I love,
   that I may meditate on your decrees.

Zayin

⁴⁹Remember your word to your servant,
   for you have given me hope.
⁵⁰My comfort in my suffering is this:
   Your promise preserves my life.

⁵¹ The arrogant mock me unmercifully,
   but I do not turn from your law.
⁵² I remember, Lord, your ancient laws,
   and I find comfort in them.
⁵³ Indignation grips me because of the wicked,
   who have forsaken your law.
⁵⁴ Your decrees are the theme of my song
   wherever I lodge.
⁵⁵ In the night, Lord, I remember your name,
   that I may keep your law.
⁵⁶ This has been my practice:
   I obey your precepts.

Heth
⁵⁷ You are my portion, Lord;
   I have promised to obey your words.
⁵⁸ I have sought your face with all my heart;
   be gracious to me according to your promise.
⁵⁹ I have considered my ways
   and have turned my steps to your statutes.
⁶⁰ I will hasten and not delay
   to obey your commands.
⁶¹ Though the wicked bind me with ropes,
   I will not forget your law.
⁶² At midnight I rise to give you thanks
   for your righteous laws.
⁶³ I am a friend to all who fear you,
   to all who follow your precepts.
⁶⁴ The earth is filled with your love, Lord;
   teach me your decrees.

Teth

⁶⁵Do good to your servant
    according to your word, Lᴏʀᴅ.
⁶⁶Teach me knowledge and good judgment,
    for I trust your commands.
⁶⁷Before I was afflicted I went astray,
    but now I obey your word.
⁶⁸You are good, and what you do is good;
    teach me your decrees.
⁶⁹Though the arrogant have smeared me with lies,
    I keep your precepts with all my heart.
⁷⁰Their hearts are callous and unfeeling,
    but I delight in your law.
⁷¹It was good for me to be afflicted
    so that I might learn your decrees.
⁷²The law from your mouth is more precious to me
    than thousands of pieces of silver and gold.

Yodh

⁷³Your hands made me and formed me;
    give me understanding to learn your commands.
⁷⁴May those who fear you rejoice when they see me,
    for I have put my hope in your word.
⁷⁵I know, Lᴏʀᴅ, that your laws are righteous,
    and that in faithfulness you have afflicted me.
⁷⁶May your unfailing love be my comfort,
    according to your promise to your servant.
⁷⁷Let your compassion come to me that I may live,
    for your law is my delight.

78 May the arrogant be put to shame for wronging me without cause;
   but I will meditate on your precepts.
79 May those who fear you turn to me,
   those who understand your statutes.
80 May I wholeheartedly follow your decrees,
   that I may not be put to shame.

Kaph
81 My soul faints with longing for your salvation,
   but I have put my hope in your word.
82 My eyes fail, looking for your promise;
   I say, "When will you comfort me?"
83 Though I am like a wineskin in the smoke,
   I do not forget your decrees.
84 How long must your servant wait?
   When will you punish my persecutors?
85 The arrogant dig pits to trap me,
   contrary to your law.
86 All your commands are trustworthy;
   help me, for I am being persecuted without cause.
87 They almost wiped me from the earth,
   but I have not forsaken your precepts.
88 In your unfailing love preserve my life,
   that I may obey the statutes of your mouth.

Lamedh
89 Your word, Lord, is eternal;
   it stands firm in the heavens.
90 Your faithfulness continues through all generations;
   you established the earth, and it endures.

⁹¹ Your laws endure to this day,
　　for all things serve you.
⁹² If your law had not been my delight,
　　I would have perished in my affliction.
⁹³ I will never forget your precepts,
　　for by them you have preserved my life.
⁹⁴ Save me, for I am yours;
　　I have sought out your precepts.
⁹⁵ The wicked are waiting to destroy me,
　　but I will ponder your statutes.
⁹⁶ To all perfection I see a limit,
　　but your commands are boundless.

Mem
⁹⁷ Oh, how I love your law!
　　I meditate on it all day long.
⁹⁸ Your commands are always with me
　　and make me wiser than my enemies.
⁹⁹ I have more insight than all my teachers,
　　for I meditate on your statutes.
¹⁰⁰ I have more understanding than the elders,
　　for I obey your precepts.
¹⁰¹ I have kept my feet from every evil path
　　so that I might obey your word.
¹⁰² I have not departed from your laws,
　　for you yourself have taught me.
¹⁰³ How sweet are your words to my taste,
　　sweeter than honey to my mouth!
¹⁰⁴ I gain understanding from your precepts;
　　therefore I hate every wrong path.

Nun

105 Your word is a lamp for my feet,
   a light on my path.
106 I have taken an oath and confirmed it,
   that I will follow your righteous laws.
107 I have suffered much;
   preserve my life, LORD, according to your word.
108 Accept, LORD, the willing praise of my mouth,
   and teach me your laws.
109 Though I constantly take my life in my hands,
   I will not forget your law.
110 The wicked have set a snare for me,
   but I have not strayed from your precepts.
111 Your statutes are my heritage forever;
   they are the joy of my heart.
112 My heart is set on keeping your decrees
   to the very end.[d]

Samekh

113 I hate double-minded people,
   but I love your law.
114 You are my refuge and my shield;
   I have put my hope in your word.
115 Away from me, you evildoers,
   that I may keep the commands of my God!
116 Sustain me, my God, according to your promise, and I will live;
   do not let my hopes be dashed.
117 Uphold me, and I will be delivered;
   I will always have regard for your decrees.

118 You reject all who stray from your decrees,
for their delusions come to nothing.
119 All the wicked of the earth you discard like dross;
therefore I love your statutes.
120 My flesh trembles in fear of you;
I stand in awe of your laws.

Ayin
121 I have done what is righteous and just;
do not leave me to my oppressors.
122 Ensure your servant's well-being;
do not let the arrogant oppress me.
123 My eyes fail, looking for your salvation,
looking for your righteous promise.
124 Deal with your servant according to your love
and teach me your decrees.
125 I am your servant; give me discernment
that I may understand your statutes.
126 It is time for you to act, Lord;
your law is being broken.
127 Because I love your commands
more than gold, more than pure gold,
128 and because I consider all your precepts right,
I hate every wrong path.

Pe
129 Your statutes are wonderful;
therefore I obey them.
130 The unfolding of your words gives light;
it gives understanding to the simple.

131 *I open my mouth and pant,*
    longing for your commands.
132 *Turn to me and have mercy on me,*
    as you always do to those who love your name.
133 *Direct my footsteps according to your word;*
    let no sin rule over me.
134 *Redeem me from human oppression,*
    that I may obey your precepts.
135 *Make your face shine on your servant*
    and teach me your decrees.
136 *Streams of tears flow from my eyes,*
    for your law is not obeyed.

Tsadhe
137 *You are righteous, LORD,*
    and your laws are right.
138 *The statutes you have laid down are righteous;*
    they are fully trustworthy.
139 *My zeal wears me out,*
    for my enemies ignore your words.
140 *Your promises have been thoroughly tested,*
    and your servant loves them.
141 *Though I am lowly and despised,*
    I do not forget your precepts.
142 *Your righteousness is everlasting*
    and your law is true.
143 *Trouble and distress have come upon me,*
    but your commands give me delight.
144 *Your statutes are always righteous;*
    give me understanding that I may live.

Qoph

145 I call with all my heart; answer me, LORD,
    and I will obey your decrees.
146 I call out to you; save me
    and I will keep your statutes.
147 I rise before dawn and cry for help;
    I have put my hope in your word.
148 My eyes stay open through the watches of the night,
    that I may meditate on your promises.
149 Hear my voice in accordance with your love;
    preserve my life, LORD, according to your laws.
150 Those who devise wicked schemes are near,
    but they are far from your law.
151 Yet you are near, LORD,
    and all your commands are true.
152 Long ago I learned from your statutes
    that you established them to last forever.

Resh

153 Look on my suffering and deliver me,
    for I have not forgotten your law.
154 Defend my cause and redeem me;
    preserve my life according to your promise.
155 Salvation is far from the wicked,
    for they do not seek out your decrees.
156 Your compassion, LORD, is great;
    preserve my life according to your laws.
157 Many are the foes who persecute me,
    but I have not turned from your statutes.

¹⁵⁸ I·look on the faithless with loathing,

    for they do not obey your word.

¹⁵⁹ See how I love your precepts;

    preserve my life, LORD, in accordance with your love.

¹⁶⁰ All your words are true;

    all your righteous laws are eternal.

Sin and Shin

¹⁶¹ Rulers persecute me without cause,

    but my heart trembles at your word.

¹⁶² I rejoice in your promise

    like one who finds great spoil.

¹⁶³ I hate and detest falsehood

    but I love your law.

¹⁶⁴ Seven times a day I praise you

    for your righteous laws.

¹⁶⁵ Great peace have those who love your law,

    and nothing can make them stumble.

¹⁶⁶ I wait for your salvation, LORD,

    and I follow your commands.

¹⁶⁷ I obey your statutes,

    for I love them greatly.

¹⁶⁸ I obey your precepts and your statutes,

    for all my ways are known to you.

Taw

¹⁶⁹ May my cry come before you, LORD;

    give me understanding according to your word.

¹⁷⁰ May my supplication come before you;

    deliver me according to your promise.

171 May my lips overflow with praise,
   for you teach me your decrees.
172 May my tongue sing of your word,
   for all your commands are righteous.
173 May your hand be ready to help me,
   for I have chosen your precepts.
174 I long for your salvation, LORD,
   and your law gives me delight.
175 Let me live that I may praise you,
   and may your laws sustain me.
176 I have strayed like a lost sheep.
   Seek your servant,
   for I have not forgotten your commands.

Stone Four: Word (God's)

I am stonked. That is stoned (in a sling kind of way) and stoked all at the same time. Nothing gets me fired up like devouring the living, breathing, and life-giving Truth of God's Word. Once your spirit tastes the power of the living water, nothing else will quench your thirst. You notice that in order to understand and study all the other stones, you have to use scripture, God's Word. All of Christianity finds its core values, precepts, and principles that it holds as truth in the Bible. It would be impossible for me to give the precepts and attributes of the other stones without using scripture. It is the same with every aspect of our lives. It only makes sense as it relates to the Bible.

As we move into the New Testament from the Old Testament, we find a really cool thing. Jesus comes on the scene and guess what? He is called the Word.

John 1:1–5, 14—The Word Became Flesh

> *¹In the beginning was the Word, and the Word was with God, and the Word was God. ²He was with God in the beginning. ³Through him all things were made; without him nothing was made that has been made. ⁴In him was life, and that life was the light of all mankind. ⁵The light shines in the darkness, and the darkness has not overcome[a] it... ¹⁴The Word became flesh and made his dwelling among us. We have seen his glory, the glory of the one and only Son, who came from the Father, full of grace and truth.*

Not only was Jesus sent to man in the flesh, but he is the Word, sent to man to fulfill what was foretold in the Old Testament. When we receive Him into our hearts, we receive the Word in our spirits. That is why it is critical for us to maintain our constant supply of God's written Word into our spirits. It completes the connection with Jesus being the living Word and residing in our hearts.

Benefits of Scripture

There is no better way to learn the benefits of having the stone of Word in our lives than examining the scriptures themselves. Meditate on the following scriptures of God's Word so that the stone of Word begins to take root in your lives and creates a solid foundation.

2 Timothy 3:14–17

> *¹⁴But as for you, continue in what you have learned and have become convinced of, because you know those from whom you learned it, ¹⁵and how from infancy you have known the Holy Scriptures, which are able to make you wise for salvation through faith in Christ Jesus. ¹⁶All Scripture is God-breathed and is useful for teaching, rebuking, correcting and training in righteousness, ¹⁷so that the servant of God may be thoroughly equipped for every good work.*

Hebrews 4:12

^{12}For the word of God is alive and active. Sharper than any double-edged sword, it penetrates even to dividing soul and spirit, joints and marrow; it judges the thoughts and attitudes of the heart.

Mark 13:31

^{31}Heaven and earth will pass away, but my words will never pass away

Psalm 1:1–3

^{1}Blessed is the one
   who does not walk in step with the wicked
or stand in the way that sinners take
   or sit in the company of mockers,
^{2}but whose delight is in the law of the LORD,
   and who meditates on his law day and night.
^{3}That person is like a tree planted by streams of water,
   which yields its fruit in season
and whose leaf does not wither—
   whatever they do prospers.

Joshua 1:8

^{8}Keep this Book of the Law always on your lips; meditate on it day and night, so that you may be careful to do everything written in it. Then you will be prosperous and successful.

Proverbs 30:5

^{5}"Every word of God is flawless;
   he is a shield to those who take refuge in him.

2 Timothy 2:15

> [15]*Do your best to present yourself to God as one approved, a worker who does not need to be ashamed and who correctly handles the word of truth.*

Revelation 19:11–13
The Heavenly Warrior Defeats the Beast

> [11]*I saw heaven standing open and there before me was a white horse, whose rider is called Faithful and True. With justice he judges and wages war.* [12]*His eyes are like blazing fire, and on his head are many crowns. He has a name written on him that no one knows but he himself.* [13]*He is dressed in a robe dipped in blood, and his name is the Word of God.*

Wow. The heavenly warrior who defeats the beast is called the **Word of God**! If that doesn't get you digging in the Word, I don't know what will. Warriors, arm yourselves with the Word of God and go forth and conquer the enemy, cover your family, and be an example of His Word to the world. Go sling the stone of Word with the power of Jesus Christ in your heart and under the guidance of the Holy Spirit.

Stone in Fright

I remember vividly the first time that I felt I was going to die. I was twelve years old and lost in the Gore Wilderness Area. I had gotten separated from the group that I was backpacking with and had no idea where I was. All I knew was that I wanted to be home…safe and out of the harsh elements of the high country.

"Dad!! Mom!! HELP!!" I yelled.

It was in vain, really, because they weren't even there. I had no idea where I was. I had gotten miserably lost. Separated from my pack, my food, and my companions, I was making every mistake that could be made. Thinking back on it today, it is a wonder that I didn't die. I can still remember the feeling of lostness: aloneness and fear. I kept walking in circles, doubling back, thinking I would recognize a place on the trail, only to get lost again and again. Then something happened that would forever change me...

Stone in Flight

In my struggle for breath, I patted my chest and felt something in my shirt pocket. Reaching into it, I felt a small, brown Gideon Bible that my Dad had given me a couple of months earlier. Our family had become followers of Jesus only months before, and Dad had given me the little Bible. I am holding it in my hand as I write this piece. I stopped there on the trail (which was a good survival move), took out the Word of God, and thumbed through it. I saw that my Dad had highlighted some verses which I may have read before, but they were about to come alive in a new way. He had highlighted John 3:16:

> *"For God so loved the world that He gave His only Son. That whoever believes in Him will not perish, but have everlasting life."*

Although I had asked Jesus into my heart months before, I knew that I was in a situation that could have ended in my perishing—at least physically—so I felt that this verse applied to me right then and there. I had hope at 12,000 feet. I then looked at the next verse that Dad had highlighted. Romans 10:13:

> *"For whoever will call on the name of the Lord will be saved."*

Now I knew that I had been spiritually saved, but I still wanted to live a while longer. At least long enough to get a driver's license. So I applied the Word and called on the name of the Lord to save me from my predicament. I did not want to perish up there in the high country, and I wanted to be saved from being lost . . . literally.

Well, obviously you know the end of the story, because I am writing to you now. I miraculously walked out of some thick, dangerous, lion- and bear-infested wilderness, living to tell the story and committing my life to doing so. You can't convince me that anything but the power of slinging God's Word saved me physically that day, just as it had done spiritually a few months earlier. I think it was ironic that I pulled the small New Testament from my pocket which was just over my heart. Yeah, you get it. It was the written Word over my heart which had accepted the living Word. I know the word *heart* we use does not mean my physical heart, but I think it is a great analogy of how the written Word of scripture and the living Word of Jesus work hand in hand.

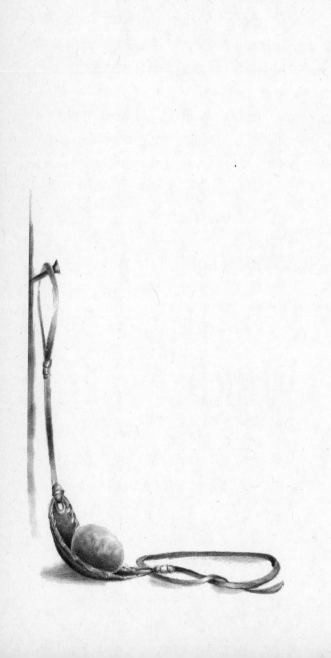

CAVE NINE

SLING TIME: WORD

This is Sling Time. We learned about the principles and precepts of the Word stone. You have to study the written Word, have the living Word of Jesus in your life, and the power and counsel of the Holy Spirit active in your life. You are a man of your word, built on the foundation of God's Word. You are now ready to put the stone of Word in your sling so it can become the foundational stone for all other stones. You will be a Wall of Word. This cave is all about slinging. Word in flight. It's also all about doing. All of your Word stones will not meet their marks, and that is okay. I want you to become so hungry for God's Word that you reach for it just like you would a glass of water when you are thirsty. The point is when you do it, you will get better.

This is where you become the writer. You are the one who fills these pages with the hieroglyphics of your CaveTime. These tell your story of using the stone of Word. The pictures and words are yours. Don't go to the next stone without putting into practice this stone. It is the power for all you do. You don't have to have to memorize the whole Bible in this cave. That will take a lifetime. This is about creating a lifestyle built on the Word. Be a doer of the Word.

Group Note

If you are doing this book as a group or FireTeam, use the time together to share your experiences—good and bad, happy and sad—during Sling Time.

What new did you learn about the stone of Word?

What ideas do you have to incorporate the stone of Word into your lifestyle and CaveTime?

_____

_____

_____

_____

_____

_____

_____

_____

_____

_____

_____

_____

_____

_____

_____

What were several scriptures that stood out to you?

_____

_____

_____

_____

_____

_____

_____

_____

_____

_____

_____

_____

_____

_____

_____

_____

What do you feel God is telling you about His Word?

_____

_____

_____

_____

_____

_____

_____

_____

_____

_____

_____

_____

_____

_____

_____

_____

Pick a scripture(s) to read over your family.

_____

_____

_____

_____

_____

_____

_____

_____

_____

_____

_____

_____

_____

Pick a scripture(s) to read over your future.

_____

_____

_____

_____

_____

_____

_____

_____

_____

_____

_____

_____

_____

_____

_____

Defeats of Sling Time

Victories of Sling Time

_____

_____

_____

_____

_____

_____

_____

_____

_____

_____

_____

_____

_____

_____

_____

_____

Practices to make this stone a part of my life

Other thoughts or scriptures

COMMUNITY

" When King David and the four hundred indebted, distressed, and discontented men gathered in the cave in 1 Samuel 22, they were anything but a mighty fighting machine. They were mighty scared, mighty broke, and mighty wanted by the law. But over time they got some stones.

They Showed Up, Worshipped, Prayed, heard, spoke God's Word, and were together. There's something powerful about being together with a band of brothers. While I believe that every man has in his DNA the ability to stand alone from time to time, I also believe (as we have already stated) that men were created to be relational. The men who entered the cave in 1 Samuel 22 were totally and miraculously changed by the time 1 Samuel 25:15 rolls around. The people who observed them said, "These men were very good to us. They did not mistreat us, and the whole time we were out in the fields near them, nothing was missing. Night and day they were a wall around us."

I challenge you, as a man, to get some Stones and learn how to use them. Show Up, Worship, Pray, read the Word, and seek out a group of brothers. **"**

CAVE TEN

STONE TIME: COMMUNITY

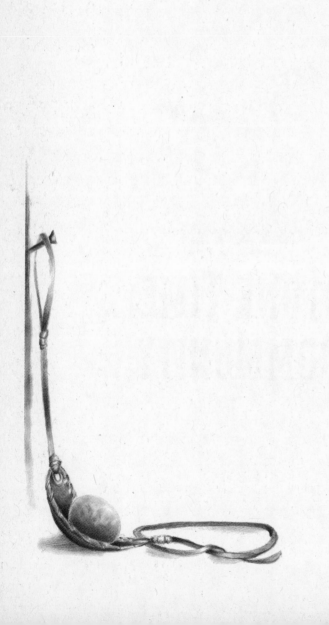

Group Note

Show the video clip of the Community stone. Have everyone read the following principles and discuss their thoughts and challenges. Discuss which areas you need to focus on in Sling Time for the stone.

Stone Five, the last stone in your sling bag, is Community. Cave mates, Band of Brothers, comrades, and friends all describe community. The ones you go to war for and those who go to war for you. The ones you share the foxholes of battle with and choose to do life with. That is your community. In many ways this is my favorite stone and defines what CaveTime really is. David entered the cave alone but emerged with those he had shared his life with. They were the men he built relationships with and whom he called friends.

Dressed to Kill—War Zone

The enemy of your soul is a liar. His whole existence is to lie, maim, and destroy you. John 10:10 says it best:

> [10] The thief comes only to steal and kill and destroy; I have come that they may have life, and have it to the full.

So what is the best way for him to do that? Separate you. Get you alone. Remove you from the herd. That is how all of nature works. If you are with the herd, your safety is multiplied. If you stray from the confines of your mates, you expose yourself to those who prey on the weak and dying. We have all seen it on the nature shows. The one that gets singled out, the one that has no backup, ends up on the predator's dinner table. They get eaten. Don't be that person. Funny thing how nature works. We always think that it is only the weak, young, and injured that get singled out and end up on the lion's or coyote's dinner table. It's true much of the time, but not all of the time. Often it is the one who thinks he is so strong and so bold that he does not need the rest of the herd to protect him. He is invincible. He is the lead bull, weighs more than all of his other herd mates, and can face anything. Really? This is called stupid. Do you get where I'm going? Not one of us can stand alone for long. Sometimes yes, but all the time no.

I have a good friend who lives on a ranch and gets to watch nature up close every day. We live in Oklahoma where coyotes abound. The more civilization grows, the more they grow in population. The coyotes have learned not only to adapt to human expansion, they have learned to exploit it. They will send a sentinel coyot (Okie slang) out in the open range to lure a domestic dog to chase it. It will act hurt or weak, giving the impression that it would be easy prey. Dogs are bred to chase, retrieve, and protect. My friend has hunting dogs, and he has to train them not to pursue the coyot. He has watched a strong but inexperienced dog take the bait and get lured into chasing the coyot. The coyot will head back into the woods and stay just far enough ahead of the dog to keep it coming. Since the dog is strong and used to getting what he chases, he continues. I don't care how strong your retriever is, his stamina is no match for the coyot in his own territory. While the sentinel coyot is luring the dog deeper into the wilderness, his unseen pack mates following in the shadows. When the strong but inexperienced dog finally chases himself into exhaustion, the sentinel coyot turns, calls his pack mates, and turns the strong, invincible retriever into their next meal.

Don't be that stupid dog that goes it alone. Learn from the pack of coyotes that know that real power is in numbers. You need cave mates to cover your backside, front side, and keep your enemy at bay. God created you for fellowship with Him and with others. Your band of brothers is your covering. They are what protect you. When the enemy lies to you, they speak truth. When you veer towards sin, they course correct you. When they are weak, you are strong for them; when you are weak, they stand over you, swords drawn to keep your enemy at bay. Together—and only together—you are dressed to kill.

Study Scripture
Proverbs 18:24

> [24] *One who has unreliable friends soon comes to ruin,*
>   *but there is a friend who sticks closer than a brother.*

I did not grow up with brothers. It was hard for me to understand how someone who was not a blood brother could be closer than a birth brother until I began to understand the code of the cave. When you think about it, you have no choice in who your blood brother is. That choice had more to do with your parents and maybe a long winter blizzard when your dad couldn't go to work for a week. A brother in the spirit, however, chooses you. You choose him. The bond is spiritual and the union of commitment more powerful than that of the flesh alone.

They say if a man can look back over his life and really have one good, loyal friend, he is ahead of most people. For whatever reason, men seem to struggle with intimacy and bonding more than women. I think it is because we are masters at wearing masks. If we let others in, they might find out who we really are, be disappointed, and cut deeper the wounds that are already there. Let us live by the creed of No Masks. You are worthy for someone to know you. If you want a friend, be a friend. Let's be honest. None of us are all that, so let's live out our days in truthfulness and unity and be a friend who sticks closer than a brother.

Stone Five: Community

The enemy wants you isolated. God wants you in the presence of others. Exact opposites. As a pastor, I deal with people and the loads they carry almost every day. Whenever a woman or man falls to the demonic attack of infidelity, there is at least one common denominator: isolation. They fall for or choose dark over light, and suddenly they find what was hidden in the dark brought to the light of day. They dropped out of church, started skipping their life group or Bible study, quit the ball team, etc. They removed themselves from their covering and their accountability.

I love the armed forces of America, but hated the Army's slogan for many years: *ARMY OF ONE.* There is no such thing. For every pair of boots on the ground, there are ten behind the scenes, running the machine to keep them there. *Army of One* is such a misnomer. Hear this: A chain is made up of many links. Put together they are a strong and powerful force. They work together to accomplish a task of pulling a load. Alone it breaks under the strain of the load, but linked together it holds and pulls with ease.

One of my favorite passages in the Bible comes from the Old Testament in the book of Ecclesiastes, chapter 4.

Ecclesiastes 4
Friendlessness

> *7 Again I saw something meaningless under the sun:*
> *8 There was a man all alone;*
>   *he had neither son nor brother.*
> *There was no end to his toil,*
>   *yet his eyes were not content with his wealth.*
> *"For whom am I toiling," he asked,*
>   *"and why am I depriving myself of enjoyment?"*
> *This too is meaningless—*
>   *a miserable business!*
> *9 Two are better than one,*
>   *because they have a good return for their labor:*

¹⁰If either of them falls down,
  one can help the other up.
But pity anyone who falls
  and has no one to help them up.
¹¹Also, if two lie down together, they will keep warm.
  But how can one keep warm alone?
¹²Though one may be overpowered,
  two can defend themselves.
A cord of three strands is not quickly broken.

I love how verse twelve puts it. One may be overpowered or defeated, but two can defend themselves. I like to think of the three-stranded cord as myself, my brother, and our God. Deadly combination, don't you think?

The Power of Next

The person next to you will make an indelible mark upon your soul. This is why we must be careful who we allow to be next to us and who we are next to. John Locke says it this way:

We are like chameleons; we take our hue and the color of our moral character from those who are around us.

Jesus did not pick the most powerful or influential people into his inner circle. He chose those who were on the fringe of society. He avoided the most powerful religious leaders and hung out with stinky fishermen, tax collectors, and laborers. Society says to do it the other way. Choose your companions for what they can do for you. I say no. Choose your companions for what you can do together. Jesus chose his band of brothers based on their hearts, their character, their loyalty, and their commitment to the rebellious ideas He knew would turn the world upside down. Who stands next to you? Who is in your inner circle? Who holds the power of YOUR life or death in his hands? Your cave mates will influence your life. Choose wisely.

Those who have served in the military throughout the ages have understood the principle of the "power of next." When the decisions of those around you often determine whether you live or die, a bond like no other is created. In 1993 an elite group of American Rangers and Delta Force soldiers were sent into war-torn Somalia. Their mission was to capture a warlord whose power-hungry regime had cost the country hundreds of thousands of lives. Saddled with faulty local intelligence and unfamiliar with the backstreets of Mogadishu, the elite force found themselves in a war they didn't understand and in a battle they could not win. I remember watching the news as the rebels dragged the body of an American solider through the streets. The 2001 Academy Award-winning movie *Black Hawk Down* was based on the bravery, camaraderie, and terrible events gone wrong during this mission. At the end of the movie after the loss of many comrades, a young Ranger asks a veteran Delta Force cohort why he was preparing to go back into the death trap the backstreets of Mogadishu had become. His response: "There are still men out there. When I go home, people ask me, 'Hey Hoot, why do you do it man, why? Are you some kind of war junkie?' I won't say a g-——-n word. Why? They won't understand. They won't understand why we do it. They won't understand it's about the men *next to* you. That's it. That's all it is."[8]

Those who you allow into your inner circle must be companions of trust, honor, duty, integrity, and courage. You must know they are with you in war and peace. We all are developed and shaped in part by the warriors we allow to fight by our sides.

Solomon learned this truth from his father and had it right when he said that "he who walks with the wise grows wise, but a companion of fools suffers harm" (Proverbs 13:20). Your closest friends—the ones who speak into your life, the ones you allow to enter into the inner chamber of your heart—must be the kind of people who will cover your back and contribute positively to your life.

The Paraclete

The term paraclete is a Greek military term that loosely translates into *one who has your back*. Greek soldiers were assigned a paraclete. They fought back-to-back, slept back-to-back, and were constant companions. Do you get the idea? Your enemy could not attack you from behind because your paraclete watched your back. You guarded him, and he guarded you. That is what the cave is all about, my friends. Protect, honor, and serve one another. Who has your back? Whose back are you guarding? Again, I say choose well. Your very life depends on it.

I love it that God's Word uses the word paraclete to define the role of the Holy Spirit or Jesus in our lives. The early church identifies our paraclete as the Holy Spirit. Right after the crucifixion of Christ, the disciples—those who were next to Jesus—were distraught and wondering what to do. During Christ's appearance to them in the upper room, He tells them that He will send another to take His place. In that moment of despair, loss, and wonder, God sends them another paraclete.

Acts 1:4–5

> 4On one occasion, while he was eating with them, he gave them this command: "Do not leave Jerusalem, but wait for the gift my Father promised, which you have heard me speak about. 5For John baptized with[a] water, but in a few days you will be baptized with[b] the Holy Spirit."

Jesus says He is sending the Holy Spirit. Paraclete here translates into English as counselor, helper, encourager, advocate, or comforter. He not only protects but also comforts us in our time of need. He helps us when we need help. He encourages us when we feel all is lost and the enemy of our soul whispers lies in our ears. He is our advocate to all voices that speak against us. Wow. What an awesome gift the Holy Spirit is for us. During his period as a hermit in the mid-12th century, Peter Abelard dedicated his chapel to the paraclete because of the comfort and grace he experienced there. He states, "I had come there as a fugitive and, in the depths of my despair, was granted some comfort by the grace of God."[9]

Isn't that what the cave is about? It is a place of refuge, healing, comfort, encouragement, and safety. It is a haven not just because of your God, but due to the men that gather there. Community forged in the fires of despair in the cave becomes the weapon we use when we are outside of the cave. I don't think you heard me. I said the pain and travail that bleed from the wounds of life onto the floor of the cave become the fuel that feeds the fire of commitment and honor that sever the heads from the beasts of hell. You're no good, you don't qualify, you're a failure, you messed up . . . all get beheaded by the ones who stand by you as your paraclete. Now do you hear me? Get that sling out, brothers. Let me hear the whistle in the wind of thousands of slings spinning over the heads of slingers, vanquishing the enemy on behalf of their cave mates.

The Arena

One of my all-time favorite movies is *Gladiator.* One of the greatest scenes comes when Maximus is leading the ragtag group of slaves—not warriors— into the belly of death in the heart of Rome known as the Colosseum. The scene is set for them to face certain death, and they decide that whatever happens in the arena, they must stick together.

> **Cassius:** On this day, we reach back to hallowed antiquity, to bring you a recreation of the second fall of the mighty Carthage! . . . On the barren plain of Zama, there stood the invincible armies of the barbarian Hannibal. Ferocious mercenaries and warriors from all brute nations, bent on merciless destruction, conquest. Your emperor is pleased to give you the barbarian horde!
>
> *[Crowd cheers]*

Maximus: *[while Cassius continues his introduction]* Anyone here been in the army?

[An unknown gladiator responds yes and tells Maximus he served under his command at Vindobona]

Maximus: You can help me. Whatever comes out of these gates, we've got a better chance of survival if we work together. Do you understand? If we stay together we survive.[10]

History has them losing the battle. All odds are against them. However all was not written. Together they refused to fight as individuals and faced their enemy together. Remember how they were chained together? A perfect picture of being each other's paraclete, don't you think?

My friend wrote the following poem that I think signifies the value of friendship forged in the arena of life.

The Arena of Life

Our arena is the place where we take our stand for all the world to see. Its walls scarred with the battles of life that we have fought. Its floor stained with the blood of the wounds we have received. Its honor shown with those we have chosen to stand beside, and its victories written on the hearts of the band of brothers that stand there.

When you fall or are wounded from the battles of the day, we are your comrades and fellow soldiers. We will surround you and protect you from life's enemies, for we are your companions, your paracletes. If you are unable to draw your sword, do not fear. For we will stand over you and declare to your enemy, "Not now. Not ever!" We guard you as surely as you guard us. Your battle is our battle, and your enemy is ours.

You will not be left behind. May our friendship be a testimony to the battles we have fought, the walls that we have built, and the caves that we have shared. We have seen victory snatched from the certainty of defeat, and we have sipped from the cup of friendship that is reserved only for those who stand and face the waning sun setting on the battlefield of life.

Our bond has been forged in the heat of the moment, when warriors lose all sense of consciousness of their surroundings except for the purpose of protecting each other and building God's kingdom. I am about you; for you are next to me.

May the holes and tears in the banner under which we fight be a testimony of our love and covenant with each other even when we fall and fail. May all we do be birthed from our friendship, trust, and loyalty.

Stay close, my brother, for many have forgotten that they are Warriors of the Way and have left their arenas. They feel they have been disqualified, that they are no longer able to fight the fight or represent the colors under which we stand. We, a band of warrior brothers, will lead them back to their arenas in which their victory and destiny await.

Your battle is my battle, your wound and victory mine, and when we get to eternity where all that matters in this life is written, may the halls echo not with our names, but with the eternal victories won because we chose to stand together in the arena of life and call each other friend.

—Jake Jones

Now that makes me ready to go to battle for my band of brothers! How about you? Now don't you see the value of the stone of Community?

Stone in Fright

It is really hard to fall to the temptations of sin when you are held accountable to others. I have been a pastor for over twenty years, and it is always
the same. A guy starts becoming more distant, drops out of touch with the
body, and before you know it, BAM. Extramarital affair, pornography, and other
addictions happen. I am not talking about slipping or falling down. I am talking
about falling off the cliff. Don't get me wrong; stuff happens to the best of us.
I am talking about hiding stuff in the dark. If you don't want to be tempted
by pornography, put a program on your computer that holds you accountable
to a cave mate. There is accountability in the cave to resist temptations and
comfort for those who are going through the fires of life. Don't be that dog
that gets lured into the woods by Wile E. Coyote. Don't be a lone ranger. Be
a part of a team. T.E.A.M. Together Everyone Accomplishes More. There is
safety, power, and victory in the herd. Stay close, my brother, so we might
guard each other.

Stone in Flight

Several years ago we had some unbelievable fires here in Oklahoma. They
burned over 60,000 acres in Creek County alone along with over four hundred
homes. With two years of drought and July temperatures hovering between
112–115 degrees, all we needed for the perfect storm was high wind. Guess
what we got? High wind. The fires were absolutely uncontrollable. With over
two hundred agencies responding, thousands of fire fighters were standing
shoulder-to-shoulder, trying to save what they could. I will never forget the
news clips of firefighters running just steps ahead of the flames that were
chasing them. Trees, houses, and cars were exploding like bombs as the heat
intensified and consumed all that was in its path.

I have a friend whose place was less than two miles from what they were
calling ground zero. With mandatory evacuations in that area, it was considered

the red zone. No one but emergency personnel got in or out. The roads were blocked, and armed patrols monitored the perimeter, keeping gawkers and looters at bay. My friend was inside the red zone, standing between his cattle, hay, house, and a wall of fire that filled the horizon and sky. I don't exactly remember who called him or who he called, but within hours, there were brothers at his place digging fire breaks and watering down the roof and hay. Remember, it was inside the red zone, and the roads were blocked with armed guards. I still don't know how we all got through, but our brother needed us. Some of the guys piled in the back of a pickup and tailgated NASCAR-style right through the barricades. Rednecks are notorious for this kind of stuff and are great to have in the cave. (Side note—Act like you know what you are doing and that you belong, even when you don't. Chances are no one will notice.) We stood with him for two days. We were a wall around him as we stared the wall of fire in the face. All for one and one for all, as the musketeers said. That is what community does. You lose all thought of self-preservation and only focus on the need of your brother. We were stones in flight those days...and it felt so good.

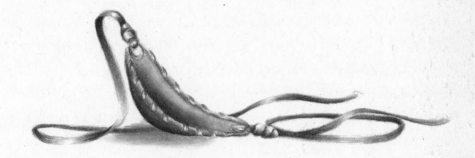

CAVE ELEVEN

SLING TIME: COMMUNITY

This is Sling Time. We learned about the principles and precepts of the Community stone. For some reason this is hard for many men to put into practice. I can promise you this: if you don't, you will not make it. Not you *might not* make it, but you *will not* make it. No man is an island unto himself. God created you for Community. Relationship is the currency of the kingdom. It is the oil that keeps the engine running. You are now ready to put the stone of Community in your sling. You have heard me talk about being a wall for those around you. The wall has many stones, made up of those God has put by your side and in your cave, and you also have an important role as a stone in that wall.

This cave is all about slinging. Community in flight. It's also all about doing. All of your Community stones will not meet their marks, and that is okay. Friendship is only formed through time. It is earned. Be a companion and look for those cave mates with a kindred spirit. Form a FireTeam or at least take steps towards the cave. Others will join. Remember alone you are prey, together you are predators. Pretty easy to pick between those two, don't you think?

This is where you become the writer. You are the one who fills these pages with the hieroglyphics of your CaveTime. These tell your story of using the stone of Community. The pictures and words are yours. Don't look at this as the last stone. It is the stone that reflects all the other stones. Comrades, cave mates, friends, paracletes, and band of brothers: this is our time. This is why we exist. Let's be men who live for the battle of defending our brother's honor. I am ready for the arena. Are you?

Group Note

If you are doing this book as a group or FireTeam, use the time together to share your experiences—good and bad, happy and sad—during Sling Time.

List by name those who you would consider your band of brothers.

_____

_____

_____

_____

_____

_____

_____

_____

_____

_____

_____

When is the last time that you stood for a friend
or intervened on a brother's behalf?

_____

_____

_____

_____

_____

_____

_____

_____

_____

_____

_____

_____

_____

_____

List the steps that you feel you need to take
to not be isolated and become prey.

_____

_____

_____

_____

_____

_____

_____

_____

_____

_____

_____

_____

_____

_____

_____

_____

List some ways or actions you can take to be a paraclete during this cave.

_____

_____

_____

_____

_____

_____

_____

_____

_____

_____

_____

_____

_____

_____

Defeats of Sling Time

Victories of Sling Time

Practices to make this stone a part of my life

_____

_____

_____

_____

_____

_____

_____

_____

_____

_____

_____

_____

_____

_____

_____

_____

Other thoughts or scriptures

_____

_____

_____

_____

_____

_____

_____

_____

_____

_____

_____

_____

_____

_____

_____

SLAY TIME

This last cave might take a week or a month. It really doesn't matter. It is a place for you to go over each of the stones and reflect how you can make them a part of your life. I am leaving this part unstructured since you are now the slinger. Treat it like Sling Time and use the time and space to reflect on each of the stones and write what is important to you. Where did you fright and where did you put the stone in flight? Which scriptures spoke to you, and which stone attributes are you good at or need to work on? You have several pages for each stone. Make them your own. You are now a Slinger. Improve your aim, and continue to use these stones every day. Stay in the cave, you mighty man.

YOU ARE NOW A GIANT SLAYER.

Stone One: Show Up

Stone Two: Worship

_____

_____

_____

_____

_____

_____

_____

_____

_____

_____

_____

_____

_____

_____

_____

Stone Three: Prayer

_____

_____

_____

_____

_____

_____

_____

_____

_____

_____

_____

_____

_____

_____

_____

_____

Stone Four: Word

Stone Five: Community

NOTES

1. *True Grit,* directed by Henry Hathaway (1969; Hollywood, CA: Paramount Pictures).

2. Rick Warren, *The Purpose Driven Life* (Perseus Books Group, 2003).

3. C.S. Lewis, *Mere Christianity* (New York, NY: HarperCollins, 1952).

4. Brother Lawrence, *The Practice of the Presence of God* (New Kensington, PA: Whitaker House, 1982).

5. Ibid.

6. Ibid.

7. Ibid.

8. Rick Hawkins, *The Inner Circle: The Value of Friendship, Trust, and Influence* (Sapulpa, OK: HonorNet, 2006), 2–3.

9. Betty Radice, *The Letters of Abelard and Heloise* (London: Penguin, 1973), p. 30.

10. *Gladiator,* directed by Ridley Scott (2000; Universal City, CA: Dreamworks).

About Jeff Voth

Dr. Jeff Voth has a doctorate in leadership and spiritual formation, a master's in philosophy and apologetics, and a master's in divinity. He is a university professor, lead pastor at a church that focuses on community outreach, and the founder and president of CaveTime. Jeff reveals that most of his life's advanced learning has come from time in his cave, just as David's did—a place of refuge and safety, and a place to hear God's voice and gain courage for the battle. Jeff is married to Lori, his wife of over thirty years. They have three sons, a daughter and son-in-law, and two grandchildren.

JOIN FIRESCHOOL

If you want to continue training and honing your slinging skills, you will need to swing it daily, monthly, and yearly. To help you in this effort, we have created FireSchool. FireSchool is an endless source of ammo for your sling and includes:

1. A daily devotional called *Words from the Cave*. *Words* is a combination of prayers, encouraging words, and Bible verses that are delivered to you via PDF download so that you can use them however you wish.

2. The FireTeam Guide. This is a monthly curriculum that deals with a broad spectrum of issues such as how to form your own FireTeam and how to engage in spiritual warfare on behalf of your people.

3. A download of the CaveTime Worship CD. This CD is a collection of twelve songs, written for the purpose of helping you engage in the stone of Worship.

4. A monthly "live cave" experience led by Jeff.

5. An archive of videos to encourage and equip you in each of the Five Stones of CaveTime. There are also interviews with other warriors such as authors Cliff Graham, Mike Altstiel and David Grieve.

6. A weekly FireTeam Email Update that keeps you informed of future CaveTime events, products, discount codes, and opportunities to pre-purchase books and music.

We are continually adding to this arsenal, and it is all available to you for only $10 per month. You can start receiving it immediately by going to CaveTime.org or scanning the QR code to the left.

Get the free CaveTime app. It connects you directly to FB, Twitter, Instagram, free music downloads, Prayer Wall, Jeff's "Show-Up" blog, and many other features to keep you swinging your sling.

Visit CaveTime.org

A re you ready to come to the cave? Bring all that you are, and all that you are not, and join other warriors who will be a wall for you. At CaveTime.org you can sign up for Jeff's blog, Facebook page, watch special videos, and receive encouragement from other cavemen. It is a virtual cave. All of our Bible studies, books, CaveTime manuals, and other materials are available at our virtual cave, CaveTime.org.

Schedule a CaveTime Event

T o book a CaveTime event or invite Jeff to minister at your church, please contact us at:

CaveTime.org

RESOURCES

Available wherever books are sold.

Are you under assault? Do you need an escape—a place where everything you are, and everything you are not, is acceptable? *CaveTime* is *God's Plan for Man's Escape from Life's Assaults.*

" *Regardless of who you are and what you've struggled with, report for duty and God can use you. How desperately the men in our culture need this book. Buy it. Read it. Soak it in.* "

—CLIFF GRAHAM,
author of the *Lion of War* book series,
including: *Day of War; Covenant of War; Benaiah*

A *Worship Experience* by The Brilliance is literally that—a worship experience. It was written to help you practice Stone 2–Worship. There are six unique worship songs with vocals and then instrumental tracks so that you can listen, think about your Creator, and raise your masculine voice to Him.